Chinese Cooking
For Beginners

Author: Huang Su-Huei
Collabor ator: Gloria C. Martinez
Publisher: Wei-Chuan's Cooking
Dishes Prepared by: Mr. Li Mu-tsun
Mr. Yeh Jia-Tzu
Photographer: Aki Ohno
Designers: Ken Fukuda
Shaw, Haizan
China Provided by: The Jade Tree
Typesetting : Alton Litho Printers
Printed by: International Scanner Colour Separation Inc.

ISBN:0-941676-00-5
© Copyright 1984 Huang Su-Huei. All rights reserved.

CHINESE COOKING

● **Helpful Hints** (for the preparation of Chinese Cuisine) 4
● **Table of Measurements** ·································· 4
● **Seasoning Used to Prepare Chinese Food** 5
● **Utensils Used to Prepare Chinese Dishes** 5
● **Culinary Idioms** ······························· 6

● Appetizers

大 拼 盤	Assorted appetizer plate	11
鷄 絲 沙 拉	Crispy salad with chicken	14
叉 燒 肉	Chinese roasted pork	14
脆 皮 鴨	Crispy-skin duck	15
拌 蜇 皮	Jellyfish salad	18
白 切 肉	Sliced pork with garlic topping	18
糖 酥 核桃	Crispy fried walnuts	19
糖 酥 腰果	Crispy fried cashews	19
薰 魚	Five-spice carp	19
五 香 牛 肉	Beef shank	22
鹽 水 鴨	Salty duck	22

● Soups

紫菜蛋花湯	Seaweed and flower soup	23
牛 肉 羹	Beef soup	23
什 錦 砂 鍋	Casserole soup	26
蟹肉蘆筍湯	Crab meat with asparagus soup	26
酸 辣 湯	Hot and sour soup	27
番茄蛋花羹	Tomato and egg flower soup	27

● Pork
● Beef
● Chicken

炸 鷄 塊	Fried chicken	30
鷄 絨 玫瑰	Chicken croquettes	30
茄 汁 鷄 脯	Chicken breasts with ketchup	31
杏 仁 鷄 片	Almond chicken	31
炒 鷄 丁	Stir-fried chicken	34
雙冬扒鷄翼	Chicken wings	34
五 味 鷄	Spicy chicken	35
宮 保 牛 肉	Beef with dried hot red pepper	35
紅 燒 扣 肉	Steamed bacon in soy sauce	38
青椒牛肉絲	Stir-fried beef with green peppers	38
沙茶牛肉串	Skewered beef with sa tsa chang	39
糖 醋 肉	Sweet and sour pork	39
紅燒牛肉(一)	Beef cooked in soy sauce I	42
炒 雜 碎	Chop suey	42
洋 葱 牛 肉	Stir-fried beef with onions	43
糯 米 丸 子	Pearl balls	43
玉 蘭 牛 肉	Beef with broccoli in oyster sauce	46
炸 大 排	Fried pork chops	46
紅 燒 鷄 腿	Chicken legs cooked in soy sauce	47
溜 鷄 片	Stir-fried chicken with vegetables	47
木 須 肉	Moo-shu pork	50
紅燒牛肉(二)	Beef cooked in soy sauce II	50

- **Fish**
- **Shrimp**
- **Crab**
- **Oysters**

炸 生 蠔　Deep-fried oysters...51
魚香鮮貝　Spicy scallops...51
清 蒸 蟹　Steamed crab...54
紅 燒 魚　Fish cooked in soy sauce...54
豉汁魚球　Stir-fried fish with fermented soy beans.....................54
瓦塊魚片　Spicy fish fillet...55
清 蒸 魚　Steamed fish...55
乾燒蝦仁　Shrimp with ketchup...58
三 色 蝦　Shrimp with vegetables...58
醋 辣 蝦　Sour and hot shrimp...59
芙 蓉 蝦　Shrimp foo yung...59
軟酥明蝦　Jumbo shrimp with ketchup...62
清炒蝦仁　Stir-fried shrimp...62
油 泡 蝦　Shrimp with soy sauce...63

- **Eggs**
- **Vegetables**
- **Bean Curd**

素 菜 捲　Vegetable rolls...63
拌 黃 瓜　Spicy cucumber salad...66
醋拌三絲　Carrot, cucumber, and Chinese radish salad..............66
涼拌白蘿蔔　Chinese radish salad...66
四川泡菜　Szechuan-style pickled salad...66
廣東泡菜　Cantonese pickled vegetables...67
辣 白 菜　Pickled Chinese cabbage...67
拌高麗菜　Pickled cabbage...67
泡黃瓜片　Cucumber salad...67
炒 菠 菜　Stir-fried spinach...70
炒高麗菜　Stir-fried cabbage...70
炒豆芽菜　Stir-fried bean sprouts...70
焗 三 蔬　Vegetable casserole...71
炸 茄 餅　Fried eggplant...71
箱子豆腐　Stuffed bean curd...74
芙蓉炒蛋　Egg foo yung...74
豉汁豆腐　Spicy bean curd...75
家常豆腐　Family-style bean curd...75
蒸 蛋　Steamed egg pudding...78
白菜豆腐　Chinese cabbage with bean curd.................................78
八 寶 菜　Shrimp, meat, and vegetable dish.................................79
佛手白菜　Cabbage rolls...79

- **Rice**
- **Noodles**
- **Snacks**
- **Desserts**

番茄炒飯　Fried rice with ground beef...82
咖哩炒飯　Curried fried rice...82
蛋 炒 飯　Fried rice with egg...82
燴 麵　Meat, shrimp, and noodle platter.................................83
炒 麵　Stir-fried noodles...83
壽 桃　Steamed long-life cakes...86
包 子　Tasty meat buns...87
炸 餛 飩　Fried won ton...90
餛 飩 湯　Won ton soup...90

炸 春 捲	Fried egg rolls	91
八 寶 飯	Rice pudding	94
杏 仁 豆 腐	Chinese almond jello	95
燒 賣 (一)	Shau mai I	98
燒 賣 (二)	Shau mai II	99
廣 式 月 餅	Cantonese-style moon cakes	102
豆 沙 做 法	Method for making red bean paste	102
蘇 式 月 餅	Short moon cakes I	103
杏 仁 酥	Chinese almond cookies	103
酥 餅	Short moon cakes II	103

Helpful Hints

for the preparation of Chinese Cuisine

- If rice wine is unavailable, you may substitute medium-dry or pale-dry sherry.
- Pre-soak Chinese black mushrooms:
  1. Rinse black mushrooms lightly and place them in warm water to cover until soft (about 15 minutes).
  2. Remove and discard stems; use caps as directed. (The soaking liquid may also be added to the recipe to provide added flavor and vitamins.)

Table of Measurements

1 Cup (1 C.)
236 c.c.

1 Tablespoon (1 T.)
15 c.c.

1 Teaspoon (1 t.)
5 c.c.

Seasoning Used to Prepare Chinese Food

Five kinds of seasonings are frequently used to prepare Chinese food: salt, MSG, pepper, sugar, and sesame oil. Wine, vinegar, cornstarch, and oil for frying, etc., are also necessary.

Soy sauce

Sesame oil
Vinegar

Oil for frying
(Fried Oil)

Cornstarch

Rice wine   Sugar   Salt   Black pepper

Utensils Used to Prepare Chinese Dishes

Cleavers, chopping block, spatulas, wok, and steamers are basic utensils used to prepare Chinese food. A rolling pin, for rolling dumplings, a sifter, and a hand-mixer are also used to prepare Chinese snacks. An iron skillet or frying pan may also be used to cook chinese food. Roasting, frying, steaming, and stewing are techniques used to prepare a wide variety of delicious food.

Steamer

Spatula

Wok   Strainer

Cleaver

Sifter

Chopping block   Hand mixer   Rolling pin for rolling dumplings

Culinary Idioms

Chinese cooking is a very subjective art. There are no definite quantities of any ingredients, nor any exact time limits for cooking any recipe. We encourage you to develop this art through trial and error. We have listed the basic information for the preparation of all dishes, as well as the ingredients needed; however, we encourage you to adapt the recipes to your own taste. In order that you may further understand the practice of Chinese cuisine, we give significant points and explain some expressions used often in Chinese cooking.

CLEANING

Clean the ingredients before using them, then drain and dry them thoroughly.

CUTTING

All ingredients must be cut into the same size and shape, so that the cooked food will look uniform and have the same tenderness.

PRE-SEASONING

Chicken, pork, beef, fish, and shrimp must be marinated in the prescribed sauces to enhance the taste of the food. Coat with egg white and cornstarch to increase tenderness.

MIXING

If no cooking is required, just mix the ingredients together after cutting. If ingredients have been precooked, allow them to cool, then mix them together; add sauce and serve.

STIR-FRYING

To put the material into a very hot wok over high heat and turn over and over, until done.

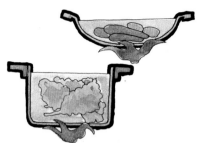

Stir-frying is a very quick process. It is advisable to prepare all of the sauces in advance, including the cornstarch and water used to thicken the final sauce.

When several kinds of ingredients are used in cooking, the difference in tenderness of each ingredient will sometimes require that material be cooked in oil, boiled, or fried before mixing. Whichever method is used, the ingredient must be precooked till tender.

When the preliminary preparation is finished, heat the wok and pour in oil. Add the onion, ginger root or garlic and stir until they impart their aroma. Add the ingredients, and a few drops of wine, if desired, to enhance the flavor of the food. Add the sauce and stir-fry until all ingredients are mixed together. This entire process must be short and quick so that the food will not overcook.

At this point, you may sprinkle a few drops of oil on the food. This will help to increase the brilliancy of the food and help to keep it warm

DEEP-FRYING

To immerse the food in deep, hot oil.

Prepare the material for frying; first the food must be marinated in the prescribed sauce, then coated with the proper flour or cornstarch batter.

There should be plenty of oil in the pan, enough to cover the material. However, if the material to be fried is very juicy or contains a lot of moisture, the oil should not occupy more than 60% of the wok so that it will not splash out of the wok.

First boil the oil; remove the wok from the heat and when the oil has cooled to medium temperature, put the food into the wok. Replace the wok over medium heat and cook until near-tender. Then turn heat to high and cook over high heat until done. This seals the flavor and ensures that the food will be completely cooked and crispy on the outside.

All food put into the oil at the same time must be removed at the same time to maintain uniformity.

STEAMING

To put the material in a 'steaming cage' which is then put on a wok containing boiling water.

First, put water in the wok and allow it to come to a boil.

Then place food in the cage and put it on the wok

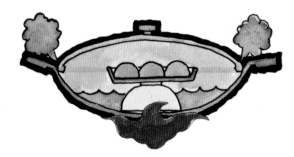

Simple method for steaming: Place a bowl, upside down, on the bottom of the wok; add water (water should not cover the bowl). Put a heatproof plate on the bowl and place food on the heatproof plate, cover and steam.

MIX-BOIL

First, put the sauce or soup into the wok by itself and allow it to boil, then add the food. The amount of cornstarch in the sauce should be to your own taste; however, there should not be too much sauce.

STEWING

Stewing is similar to steaming. Put water in a large pot. Put material and water or stock, to cover, in a smaller pot and set it inside the large pot. Cook over a moderate heat until the food is tender. Soup prepared this way is very clear.

SMOKING

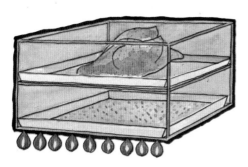

Put food in an oven (or cover and place on a grill); throw sugar, wood powder, or tea leaves into the fire or oven so that the fumes will smoke the food and give it flavor.

ROASTING

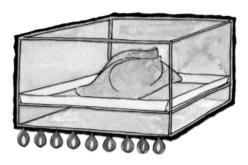

Cook or bake food in the oven with all the ingredients, until done.

PRECOOKING

Place ingredients in hot oil or hot water for several seconds, or until slightly tender, then remove. (Pork, beef. chicken, fish, or shrimp is usually sliced or shredded, seasoned, and coated with cornstarch before precooking.)

oil out

Preparing the wok:
Heat the wok then place 4 Tbsp. oil in wok and swirl it in wok to cover lower two-thirds of surface; remove excess oil. (This will prevent ingredients from sticking.)

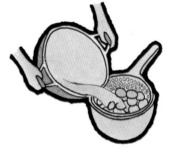

Reheat wok and add enough oil to cover ingredients; heat oil until hot but not smoking. Add food. Stir quickly to Separate ingredients; stir-fry until ingredients change color then remove. (Add 1 Tbsp. oil to ingredients and stir before frying. The ingredients will separate easily.)

STOCK

Broth from boiled Pork, beef, or chicken meat or bones.

Boil water in a large pot; add pork, beef, or chicken meat or bones to boiling water. Remove. Discard water. (Purpose: to clean the meat.)

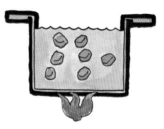

Put clean water in the pot and add the pork, beef, or chicken meat or bones. Bring to a boil and remove any scum. After removing scum, lower heat to medium. Add two green onions, two slices of ginger root, and one tablespoon wine. Cook for one hour. Remove pork, beef, or chicken. Stock is ready for use.

Assorted appetizer plate 大 拼 盤

Abalone: Use canned abalone meat.
Beef Shank: See P. 22
Ham: Use cooked ham.
Sliced Pork with Garlic Topping: See P. 18
Chinese Roasted Pork: See P. 14
Crispy Fried Walnuts: See P. 19
Salted Shrimp: Clean shrimp; place in
    salted boiling water; add a little wine
    and cook for 1 minute.

12 servings

鷄絲沙拉
Crispy salad with chicken
Salade croustillante au poulet

叉燒肉
Chinese roasted pork
Porc rôti à la chinoise

12

脆 皮 鴨
Crispy-skin duck
Canard à la peau croustillante

13

½ chicken or chicken legs (about 1⅓ lbs.)	
1½ c. shredded lettuce	

① celery, brown onion, bell pepper, pickled mustard greens — shredded to equal 3 cups, rinse

②
- 1 T. white vinegar
- ½ T. soy sauce, sesame oil
- 1 t. sugar
- ¾ t. salt

③
- 2 T. roasted, ground peanuts
- 1 T. browned sesame seeds. no oil
- 6 won ton skins
- oil for frying

❶ Boil the chicken. The skin may be removed; bone and shred. Mix ② in a bowl. Cut the won ton skins into ¼-inch strips. Heat the wok then add the oil. To test oil for readiness: Put a strip of won ton in the oil. If it stays at the bottom, the oil is not hot enough (remove the won ton). Allow more time for the oil to heat. Put another strip of won ton in the oil. The won ton will quickly surface if the oil is hot enough (remove the strip of won ton). Quickly deep-fry the strips of won ton; remove and drain.

❷ Arrange the lettuce on a serving platter. Toss ① and ② together with the shredded chicken; place them on the bed of lettuce. Sprinkle ③ and the fried won ton strips over the salad. Serve immediately so that the vegetables will remain crunchy and the won ton strips will stay crispy. Serve.

①
- 2 lbs. shoulder pork, not lean
- 3 T. sugar
- 1½ T. cooking wine, or sherry, soy sauce, hoisin sauce
- 2 t. salt

②
- 2 T. soy sauce
- 1 T. chopped garlic clove

or

③
- 2 T. soy sauce
- 1 T. hot chili paste

Two methods of cooking may be used:

- First method (easy method that is very practical for family use): Cut the pork into strips 1 inch wide; add ① and mix. Marinate for several hours or overnight (overnight preferable). Preheat the oven to 400° to 450°. Place the meat on a roasting pan and place it on the middle rack of the oven. Bake for 30 minutes; remove and serve.
- Second method: Preheat the oven to 400° to 450°. Cut the meat into slices 1/3-inch thick (Fig. 1). Add ①; marinate for several hours or overnight. Remove from the marinade. Beginning at the long edge, roll the meat (Fig. 2) and tie it with a string to hold it in place (Fig. 3). Place the meat on a roasting pan and place it on the middle rack of the oven. Bake for 1 hour; remove. Slice and serve.

■ Barbeque sauce may be substituted for ①.
■ Use either dipping sauce ② or ③ when serving.
■ This dish may be served hot or cold.

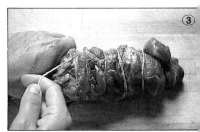

① {
1   duckling (about 4 lbs.)
1   green onion
2   slices ginger root
1   T. salt
1   t. five-spice powder
1   t. cooking wine or sherry
}

② {
10   c. water
3   T. salt
4   T. hoisin sauce
1½   T. honey
}

❶   Clean the duckling and pat it dry. Rub the exterior and cavity of the duckling with ① ; close the cavity with a toothpick or skewer (Fig. 1).

❷   Bring ② to a boil. Hold the duckling over the wok and ladle ② over the entire surface of the duckling (Fig. 2). Discard ② from the wok. Spread honey on the surface of the duckling (Fig. 3). Place (hang) the duckling in a well-ventilated place and let it dry for 12-24 hours. Touch to test for dryness. The skin must not be moist. If the duckling is baked while the skin is moist, the skin will wrinkle. If it is baked when the skin is thoroughly dry, the skin will be firm and shiny. If the duckling is allowed to dry for more than 12 hours, the skin will be crispier when baked. Preheat the oven to 450°.

❸   Put water in a shallow roasting pan and place it on the lowest rack of the oven. Place the duckling directly on the middle rack of the oven; center it over the shallow pan of water. The drippings from the duckling will fall into the pan of water and prevent its smoking and maintain the duckling's crispiness. Bake for about 20 minutes; bake both sides until they are golden brown. Lower the heat to 350°. Total baking time is about 50 minutes. Remove and cut the duckling into bite-size pieces. Serve; use hoisin sauce as a dipping sauce.

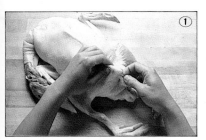  

拌 蜇 皮
Jellyfish salad
Peaux de méduse en salade

白 切 肉
Sliced pork with garlic topping
Tranches de porc à l'ail

糖 酥 核 桃
Crispy fried walnuts
Noix croustillantes

糖 酥 腰 果
Crispy fried cashews
Noix de cajou croustillantes

薫　　魚
Five-spice carp
Poisson cinq épices

17

Jellyfish salad 拌蜇皮 serves 6

⅓ lb. salted jellyfish

① { 1   T. soy sauce, white vinegar, sesame oil }
    { 1   t. sugar } mix

❶ Purchase thick, golden jellyfish (Fig. 1). Shred and wash the jellyfish. Bring 6 cups water to a boil; turn off the heat. Plunge the jellyfish into the water and stir quickly. When the jellyfish curl, remove them (Fig. 2) Plunge the jellyfish into cold water; rinse them several times until they are cold. Soak the jellyfish for 4-5 hours; change the water every hour. The jellyfish will be slightly larger and crunchy (Fig. 3). Mix with ① and serve. Shredded cucumber and/or shredded white radish may be added to the jellyfish then tossed together.

Sliced pork with garlic topping 白切肉 serves 6

1   lb. pork (Boston shoulder)

① { 10 c. water
    { 1   T. cooking wine or sherry
    { 2   green onions
    { 2   slices of ginger root

5   garlic cloves

② { 3   T. sweet bean paste
    { 1   T. soy sauce, sesame oil
    { ½   T. white vinegar
    { 1   t. sugar
    { ½   t. hot chili paste

❶ Parboil the pork in a pot of boiling water to clean; discard the water. Add ① to the pork to cover. Bring to a boil over medium heat; cook for 30 minutes. Remove the pork, retain the liquid. When the pork is cool, slice it. Reboil the retained liquid. Place the sliced pork in a strainer then dip it in the liquid to heat the meat. Remove to a serving dish.

❷ Finely chop the garlic; put it in a small bowl and mix with ②. If necessary, and stock and mix; pour over the sliced pork.

■ Pork slices may be rolled as shown in the picture.
■ The retained liquid may be used for won ton soup or for other soups.
■ Hot chili paste and sweet bean paste may be purchased at most Chinese markets.

Crispy fried walnuts 糖酥核桃 serves 6

½ lb. shelled walnuts (without skins)
① { 1 c. water
3 T. sugar
1 T. maltose or honey
oil for frying

❶ Put the nuts in ① and heat for 5 minutes over medium heat; remove and drain.
❷ Heat the wok then add the oil. Deep-fry the nuts over low heat for at least 5 minutes. Stir continuously to ensure even browning and prevent burning. Remove and drain. Allow to cool. The nuts should be crispy.
■ Shell the walnuts (Figs. 1, 2). Blanch the walnuts in boiling water to loosen the skin. Remove. Use a knife or toothpick to remove the skins (Fig. 3).

Crispy fried cashews 糖酥腰果 serves 6

½ lb. raw cashew nuts
① same as shown above
oil for frying

● Follow the directions as given for Crispy-fried walnuts. Deep-fry the nuts for 15 minutes.
■ If cashew nuts with skins are used they become very dark during frying. To remove the skin, follow the Crispy-fried walnuts.

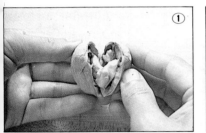  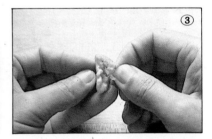

Five-spice carp 薫魚 serves 12

① {
1 yellow fish (about 1⅓ lbs.)
2 green onion, cut into 4 pieces
2 slices of ginger root
½ T. soy sauce
1½ T. cooking wine or sherry
½ t. salt
⅓ t. five-spice powder

② {
oil for frying
1 hot red pepper
2 c. water
2 T. sugar, soy sauce, cooking wine or sherry
1 t. white vinegar
1 T. sesame oil

❶ Clean the fish and pat it dry. Cut it into 1-inch slices. Mix with ① and marinate for 1 hour. Remove the fish ; retain the onion and ginger root. Before deep-frying the fish, pat it dry to remove excess marinade.
❷ Heat the wok the add oil. Deep-fry 2 or 3 slices per batch, until the skin is golden brown; remove. Deep-fry the rest of the fish. Return the fish to the wok; deep-fry for 8 minutes; remove and drain. Remove the oil from the wok.
❸ Place ②, fish, green onion, and ginger (from marinade) in the wok; bring to a boil. Turn the heat to low and cook for 15 minutes or until the liquid has almost completely evaporated. Drizzle with sesame oil. Remove to a serving plate; when cool, serve. This dish will deep for 4 or 5 days if refrigerated.
■ Carp, small yellow fish, or pomfret may be used.

19

五香牛肉
Beef shank
Bœuf-épices 5 parfums

鹽水鴨
Salty duck
Canard salé froid

20

菜蛋花湯
Seaweed and flower soup
Potage aux œufs et aux feuilles de nori

牛 肉 羹
Beef soup
Potage au bœuf

21

Beef shanks 五香牛肉

2 beef shanks (about 3 lbs.) (Fig. 1)	⑧ c. water
4 T. sugar	¾ c. soy sauce
1 T. sesame oil	① 1 T. cooking wine or sherry
	1 star anise or ¼ t. five-spice powder

- Put 6 cups of water in a large saucepan and bring it to a boil. Place the shanks in the boiling water; parboil for 1 minute to clean. Remove the shanks and rinse them with cold water (Fig. 2). Discard the water. Put the shanks in the saucepan and add ① to cover; bring to a boil. Reduce the heat to low and cook for at least 2 hours, or until they are tender. Use a chopstick to test for doneness. Add the sugar and cook for 10 minutes; the liquid will thicken slightly. Add 1 T. sesame oil. Turn off the heat; remove and allow to cool (Fig. 3). To serve, slice the desired portion then sprinkle with sesame oil. The shanks will keep for three days if refrigerated.

Salty duckling 鹽水鴨

1 duckling (about 4 lbs.)	② 10 c. water
¼ c. salt	½ c. salt, cooking wine or sherry
2 T. cooking wine or sherry	
① 2 green onions	
2 slices ginger root	
1 t. Szechuan peppercorns	

❶ Clean the duckling. Rub the exterior and cavity of the duckling with ① ; leave ① in the cavity. Refrigerate the duckling to marinate for 2 or 3 days.

❷ Bring a half pot of water to a boil. Blanch the duckling in the boiling water; remove and rinse.

❸ Bring ② to a boil; add the duckling and boil for 1 minute. Turn off the heat and cover; simmer for 10 minutes. Remove the duckling and drain it. Reboil the liquid and cook the duckling for 1 minute; turn off the heat and cover; let stand for 10 minutes. Repeat step 3 three times. Remove and drain; allow the duckling to cool then slice.

■ It is better to allow the meat to stand in the hot water to keep it salty than to boil it continuously. The duckling will keep for 3 or 4 days if refrigerated.

Seaweed and flower soup 紫菜蛋花湯 serves 6

1   sheet seaweed
3   eggs
① { 6   c. stock
     1½ t. salt

② { 2   T. chopped green onions
     dash of pepper

❶ Tear the seaweed into 2-inch squares. Lightly beat the eggs.
❷ Boil ① in a pot. Slowly add the eggs in a thin stream; stir lightly and turn off the heat. Add the seaweed and ② ; mix and serve.

Beef soup 牛肉羹 serves 6

⅓   lb. beef
① { ½   T. cornstarch, soy sauce
     1   T. water
     1   t. cooking wine or sherry
② { 6   c. stock
     1½ t. salt

③ { 4   T. cornstarch } mix
     5   T. water
④ { 3   egg whites or 2 whole eggs
     3   T. water
⑤ { 4   T. coriander } chopped
     2   T. green onions
     dash of pepper, sesame oil

❶ Slice the meat and mix with ① . Set aside for later use. Mix ③ and ④ in separate bowls. Put ⑤ in a soup bowl.
❷ Boil ② in a pot; put the meat in a strainer (the strainer should rest in the broth). Use chopsticks or a fork to separate the sliced meat (Fig. 1) then put the meat in the pot and stir. Bring to a boil. Add mixture ③ to thicken; stir (Fig. 2). Boil again. Slowly add mixture ④ in a thin stream while stirring gently (Fig. 3) then turn off the heat. Pour the mixture into a soup bowl with ⑤ ; mix and serve.

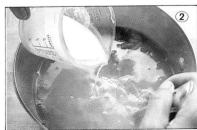

什錦砂鍋
Casserole soup
Casserole au poulet et aux choux verts

蟹肉蘆筍湯
Crab meat with asparagus soup
Soupe de crabe aux asperges

酸 辣 湯
Hot and sour soup
Soupe aigre-douce

番茄蛋花羹
Tomato and egg flower soup
Soupe de tomate aux œufs

25

炸 鶏 塊
Fried chicken
Poulet sauté

鶏 絨 玫 瑰
Chicken croquettes
Barquettes de poulet

酸　辣　湯
Hot and sour soup
Soupe aigre-douce

番茄蛋花羹
Tomato and egg flower soup
Soupe de tomate aux œufs

1	chicken leg	10	shrimp balls, or meatballs, or fish balls
6	leaves of nappa cabbage	10	shrimp
6	hearts bok choy (to include about 6 stalks)	¾	c. button mushrooms or straw mushrooms
3	dried scallops, presoftened	½	1 lb. can asparagus
6	Chinese black mushrooms, presoftened		
1	4 oz. pkg. bean threads	① 6	c. stock
2	pieces of bean curd (4 pieces in a box)	1½	t. salt

❶ Cut the chicken leg into bite-size pieces; parboil for 1 minute, to clean the meat. Discard the water. Cut the cabbage into 2-inch pieces (Fig. 1). Remove outer leaves of bok choy. Use only the heart and tender leaves; trim the thick stem (Fig. 2). Separately parboil the cabbage then bok choy for 1 minute. Remove the dark vein from the shrimp and wash carefully. Separately soak the scallops, mushrooms, and bean threads in water (Fig. 3). Cut the asparagus in half crosswise. Cut the bean curd into bite-size pieces.

❷ Place the cabbage in a casserole or heatproof dish; add all of the remaining ingredients. The stock and salt solution, ① , should cover the ingredients. Bring to a boil; turn heat to low and cook for 20 minutes.

- This dish is adaptable to your favorite vegetables.
- Shrimp balls, meatballs, or fish balls may be purchased at most Chinese markets.

1	c. crab meat, button mushrooms	① 6	c. stock	
½	c. asparagus	1½	t. salt	
⅓	c. peas, precooked	② 4	T. cornstarch	mix
2	pieces of bean curd (4 pieces in a box)	5	T. water	
		③ 2	egg whites	lightly
		2	T. water	beaten

❶ Cut the asparagus into 1-inch pieces. Slice the mushrooms. Cut the bean curd into quarters then cut them across into slices ¼" thick.

❷ Bring ① to a boil. Add the crab meat, asparagus, mushrooms, bean curd, and peas. Bring to a boil again. Add mixture ② to thicken; stir. Boil again and slowly add ③ in a thin stream; stir lightly and turn off the heat. Serve.

Hot and sour soup 酸辣湯 serves 6

2 pieces of bean curd (4 pieces in a box) cut into strips

⅔ c. shredded meat, pork, beef, or chicken

① {
½ T. cornstarch
1 T. water
½ T. soy sauce
1 t. cooking wine or sherry
}

② {
6 c. stock
1¼ t. salt
}

③ {
4 T. cornstarch
5 T. water
} mix

2 eggs

④ {
1 T. chopped coriander
3 T. white vinegar
3 T. soy sauce
2 T. green onions
2 T. ginger root
} shredded
½ t. pepper
dash of sesame oil
}

❶ Add the meat to ① ; mix and marinate for 20 minutes. Beat the eggs lightly. Put ④ in a serving soup bowl.

❷ Boil ② in a pot; put the meat in a strainer, the strainer should rest in the broth. Use chopsticks or a fork to separate the meat then put the meat in the pot. Add the bean curd and bring to a boil. Add mixture ③ to thicken; stir. Boil again. Slowly add the eggs in a thin stream; stir lightly and turn off the heat. Pour this mixture into a bowl with ④ ; mix and serve.

■ Bamboo shoot (Fig. 1), dried tiger lily blossoms (Fig. 2), shredded Chinese black mushrooms (Fig. 3), wood ears, or other vegetables may be added.

Tomato and egg flower soup 番茄蛋花羹 serves 6

① {
1 tomato, diced
1 T. chopped green onion
}
1 T. soy sauce

② {
6 c. soup stock or water
1½ t. salt
}
2 pieces of bean curd; diced (4 pieces in a box)

③ {
4 T. cornstarch
5 T. water
} mix

2 eggs, lightly beaten

④ {
2 T. chopped green onions
dash of pepper
}
3 T. oil

● Heat the wok then add 3 T. oil. Stir-fry ① over medium heat. Add 1 T. soy sauce then add ② and the bean curd; bring to a boil. Add mixture ③ to thicken; stir. Slowly add eggs in a thin stream; stir lightly and turn off the heat. Add ④ ; mix and serve.

炸 鷄 塊
Fried chicken
Poulet sauté

鷄 絨 玫 瑰
Chicken croquettes
Barquettes de poulet

28

茄汁鷄脯
Chicken breasts with ketchup
Escalopes de poulet à la sauce tomate

杏仁鷄片
Almond chicken
Escalopes de poulet aux amandes

29

Fried chicken　炸鷄塊

3	medium-size chicken legs (about 1⅓ lbs.)

① ⎰ ½ T. cooking wine or sherry
½ t. salt
½ t. sugar
2 t. soy sauce
2 green onions
2 slices ginger root

1　small egg yolk
2　T. cornstarch
oil for frying

❶ Cut the chicken legs into bite-size pieces and mix with ① . Marinate for 1 hour. Before frying, add the egg yolk and mix. Add the cornstarch then mix.

❷ Heat the wok then add the oil. Use medium heat to deep-fry the chicken for 4 minutes; remove and drain. Reheat the oil. Add the fried chicken and fry it until the skin is crispy; remove and serve.

Chicken croquettes　鷄絨玫瑰

½ lb. chicken breasts

① ⎰ 1 T. water
¼ t. salt
1 t. cooking wine or sherry

4 egg whites
1 T. cornstarch
4 radishes

② ⎰ 1 c. stock
½ t. salt
1 t. cooking wine or sherry

③ ⎰ ½ T. cornstarch
1½ T. water ⎱ mix

12 molds

❶ Remove any tendons from the chicken (Fig. 1). Chop the chicken finely then add ① . Beat the egg whites gently. Gradually pour the egg whites and mix into the chicken mixture (Fig. 2). Add 1 T. cornstarch and mix. Slice the radishes.

❷ Oil the molds then put 1 portion of chicken mixture into the mold. Arrange radish slices as shown (Fig. 3). Steam for 6 minutes over low heat; remove. Remove chicken from the molds and arrange on a serving platter.

❸ Boil ② ; add mixture ③ to thicken and stir. Pour over the chicken croquettes; serve.

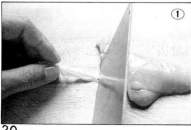

Chicken breasts with ketchup 茄汁鷄脯 **serves 6**

② lb. chicken breast or chicken legs
① {
1 T. cornstarch, soy sauce
½ T. cooking wine or sherry
⅔ c. shredded onions
}

② {
2 T. water
1 T. soy sauce
½ T. white vinegar
1½ T. ketchup
2 t. sugar
¼ t. sesame oil
}

To bone chicken breasts:
*Cut the meat along the outside of the rib cage to the spine (Fig. 1). Spread the meat away from the bone (Fig. 2). Repeat from * for the other side. Turn the breast over. While holding the two sides of the meat, cut it away from the rib cage. Pull away the rest of the meat from the neck area down (Fig. 3). See p. 34 to bone chicken legs.

❶ Laterally cut the chicken breasts into large pieces. Use a meat mallet to tenderize the meat; add ① and mix together. Marinate for 20 minutes.

❷ Heat the wok then add 2 T. oil. Fry the meat on both sides until it is golden, fry about 1½ minutes on each side. The meat should be cooked thoroughly. Move the meat aside. Add 1 T. oil and stir-fry the onions. Add ②; bring to a boil then mix together with chicken. Quickly stir-fry until thoroughly mixed; remove and serve.

Almond chicken 杏仁鷄片 **serves 6**

⅔ lb. chicken breast or chicken legs

① {
1½ T. cornstarch
½ T. cooking wine or sherry
1 t. sugar
½ t. salt
dash of pepper
1 egg white
}

1½ c. sliced almonds
oil for frying

❶ Remove the skin from the chicken. Cut the chicken breast into paper-thin slices; add ① and mix. Marinate for 20 minutes.

❷ Place the almonds in a dish; coat each slice of chicken with almonds.

❸ Heat the oil over medium heat; deep-fry the chicken for 1½ minutes. When it is cooked, the slices of chicken will rise to the surface. Remove and serve.

■ To bone chicken breast, see p. 31, Chicken breast with ketchup.

炒 鷄 丁
Stir-fried chicken
Dés de poulet sautés

雙冬扒鷄翼
Chicken wings
Ailes de poulet aux champignons parfumés et au bambou

32

五 味 鷄
Spicy chicken
Poulet 5 parfums

宮 保 牛 肉
Beef with dried hot red pepper
Bœuf mode Kong Pao

33

	3	chicken legs, boned		½	carrot, precooked
①	1	T. cornstarch, water		1	small bell pepper
	½	T. cooking wine or sherry		3	hot red peppers
	⅓	t. salt		4	T. water
	½	c. oil	②	½	T. cooking wine or sherry
	6	½-inch pieces of green onions		1	t. cornstarch
	½	T. sliced ginger root		½	t. salt, sugar
	⅔	c. button mushrooms			mix

❶ Dice the chicken legs and mix with ① . Marinate for 20 minutes.

❷ Cut the mushrooms into quarters; dice the carrot, green pepper, and red hot pepper. Mix ② in a bowl.

❸ Heat the wok then add oil. When the oil is hot put the meat in the wok. Stir-fry the meat until it changes color. Remove and drain (see p. 9 for precooking). Add 1 T. oil and stir-fry the onions and ginger root. Add the mushrooms, carrots, and peppers; stir-fry lightly. Add the chicken and ② ; quickly stir-fry. Remove and serve.

■ Other vegetables may be used or added to those listed in recipe.

■ To bone chicken legs: Make a vertical cut from the bottom of the leg to the top (Fig. 1). Cut through the joint. Remove the bone by pulling the meat away from the bone (Fig. 2). Cut off the tip of the bone at the narrow end. Hold the bone in place by lightly striking it with a knife and holding the knife (Fig. 3).

Chicken wings 雙冬扒鷄翼 serves 6

1⅓	lbs. chicken wings			1½	c. water
1	T. soy sauce			3	T. soy sauce
oil for frying			①	1½	T. cooking wine or sherry
4	black mushrooms, presoftened			2	t. sugar ·
1	precooked, or canned, bamboo shoot		②	1	T. water
				2	t. cornstarch mix

❶ Cut the chicken wings at the joint; add 1 T. soy sauce; marinate for 20 minutes. Slice the mushrooms and cut the bamboo shoot into bite-size pieces.

❷ Heat the wok then add oil. Deep-fry the chicken for 1½ minutes or until golden. Drain the oil. Put ① and the chicken in the wok. Cover and cook over medium heat. Lower the heat after it comes to a boil; cook for 10 minutes. Add the mushrooms and bamboo shoot. Cook for 10 minutes. The sauce will reduce to 2/3 cups. Slowly pour mixture ② into the wok while stirring. Remove and serve.

■ Whole chicken or chicken legs may be substituted.

① {
1	whole chicken (about 2 2/3 lbs.)
2	green onions
2	slices of ginger root
1	T. cooking wine or sherry
2	t. salt
½	c. cornstarch
10	c. water
2	egg yolks

② {
3	T. soy sauce, stock (or water)
3	T. green onions
2	T. ginger root } chopped
½	T. garlic clove
½	T. sesame oil
1	t. sugar
2	t. white vinegar

oil for frying

❶ Mix ① then rub it on the chicken. Marinate for 1 hour. Spoon ① into the cavity of the chicken. Place the chicken in a pot; add 10 c. water. (The water should be halfway up the side of the chicken.) Bring to a boil over high heat. Turn heat to low; cover and cook for 10 minutes. Turn the chicken over and cook for 10 minutes; remove and let it cool. Break the egg yolks and spread them over the chicken. Coat the chicken with cornstarch. Mix ② in a bowl.

❷ Heat the wok then add oil. Deep-fry the chicken over high heat for 6 minutes. The chicken should be crispy; drain. Cut the chicken into bite-size pieces; pour ② over the chicken and serve.

■ To cut the chicken: pull the wings away from the body of the chicken. Cut through the joint and remove the wing. Repeat for the other wing. Grasp the leg and pull it away from the body of the chicken. Cut through the meat between the thigh and backbone and separate it (Fig. 1). Remove the other leg in the same manner. Use a sharp cleaver to cut under the rib cage to remove it from the tail end to the opposite end (Fig. 2). Cut large pieces into bite-size pieces (Fig. 3).

Beef with dried hot red pepper 宮保牛肉 serves 6

① {
⅔	lb. lean beef
1	T. cornstarch
1	T. soy sauce
½	T. water
½	T. cooking wine or sherry
½	c. oil
5	dried hot red peppers, cut into pieces ½ inch long
6	½-inch pieces of green onion

② {
2½	T. soy sauce
2	T. water
1	T. cooking wine or sherry
2	t. sugar
1	t. cornstarch
1	t. white vinegar
3	T. oil

❶ Slice the meat and mix it with ① . Marinate for 20 minutes. Before frying, add 1 T. oil and mix so that the meat will separate easily during frying. Put ② in a bowl.

❷ Heat the wok then add oil. Stir-fry the meat until it changes color; remove (see p. 9 for precooking.) Add 3 T. oil; fry the hot red peppers over medium heat. Add 3 T. oil; fry the hot red peppers over medium heat. Add the onions and ② ; stir-fry lightly. Turn the heat to high. Add the beef and stir quickly; remove and serve.

紅燒扣肉
Steamed bacon in soy sauce
Estouffades de porc à la sauce de soja

青椒牛肉絲 Stir-fried beef with green peppers
Bœuf sauté au poivron

沙茶牛肉串
Skewered beef with sa tsa chang
Brochettes de bœuf

糖醋肉
Sweet and sour pork
Porc à l'ananas-sauce aigre-douce

37

Steamed bacon in soy sauce 紅燒扣肉 **serves 6**

1⅓ lbs. fresh bacon (2 inches wide)
5 T. soy sauce
oil for frying

① { 1 T. cooking wine or sherry
2 t. sugar
2 green onions
2 slices of ginger root

❶ Place the fresh bacon in a pot of water to cover; cook over medium heat for 30 minutes. Remove and pat dry. Lightly pierce the skin of the bacon to prevent big bubbles from forming during deep-frying. Pat dry the bacon then rub 5 T. soy sauce over the skin; drain and retain the soy sauce.

❷ Heat the oil for deep-frying. Deep-fry the bacon, skin side down, over medium heat for 3 minutes or until brown (cover to prevent oil from splashing). Remove and rinse in cold water. Slice the bacon (Fig. 1).

❸ Arrange the slices of pork, skin side down, in a medium-size heatproof soup bowl (Fig. 2). Pack the slices securely into the bowl; add ① and retained soy sauce. Place the onions and ginger root on top (Fig. 3). Steam over high heat for 1 hour (the pork should be very tender). Remove and put a plate, slightly larger than the steaming bowl, over the bowl. Tilt them slightly to drain the liquid; retain the liquid. Invert the bowl on a serving plate; remove the bowl. Pour the retained liquid over the pork. Serve.

■ This dish can be served with rice or bread.

Stir-fried beef with green peppers 青椒牛肉絲 **serves 6**

½ lb. beef tenderloin
① { ¾ T. cornstarch, soy sauce
½ T. cooking wine or sherry
1 T. water
½ c. oil for frying
1½ c. shredded bell pepper

② { 1 T. fermented black beans, green onions } chopped
½ T. ginger root, garlic

③ { 2 T. water
1½ t. cornstarch
1 t. sugar, salt
dash of black pepper, sesame oil

❶ Finely shred the beef across the grain and mix with ①. Before stir-frying, add 1 T. oil and mix so that the meat will separate easily during frying. Place ② and ③ in separate bowls for later use.

❷ Heat the wok then add oil. Stir-fry the beef until it changes color; remove (This is precooking, see p. 9). Remove the oil from the wok. Reheat the wok then add 1 T. oil. Add the bell pepper and 1 T. water. Stir-fry briefly; remove to a bowl for later use.

❸ Reheat the wok then add 1 T. oil. Stir-fry ② until fragrant. Add the beef, bell pepper, and ③. Turn heat to high and quickly stir to mix. Transfer to a serving plate and serve.

Skewered beef with sa tsa chang 沙茶牛肉串 serves 6

①
- ⅔ Ib. lean beef
- 1 T. soy sauce
- ½ T. cooking wine or sherry
- ½ T. water
- 1 T. cornstarch
- 1 T. oil

②
- 6 T. Sa Tsa Chang
- 1½ T. sugar
- 1 T. soy sauce
- 3 T. water
- 6 skewers

❶ Slice the beef into 1½-inch pieces. Add ① and mix well. Mix ② in a bowl for later use.

❷ Divide the sliced beef into 6 portions. Insert the sliced beef through the skewers.

❸ Heat the wok then add 1 T. oil. Add ② and bring it to a boil. Add the skewered beef and bring it to a boil again. Turn the skewered beef over. Cook for 1 minute over medium heat; remove and serve.

■ Sa Tsa Chang may be purchased at most Chinese markets.

■ Mix ② thoroughly before use; if the mixture is too thick, and water.

Sweet and sour pork 糖醋肉 serves 6

- ½ Ib. pork, beef, or chicken

①
- 1 egg yolk
- 1 T. cornstarch
- ½ T. soy sauce
- 6 T. cornstarch
- oil for frying
- ½ onion, pineapple
- 1 small bell pepper

- ½ t. chopped garlic
- 4 T. oil

②
- 3 T. sugar, water
- 2 T. pineapple juice, white vinegar
- 2 T. ketchup
- ½ t. salt

③
- 1 T. water
- 1½ t. cornstarch
} mix

❶ Cut the meat into 2/3-inch slices. Use the blunt edge of a cleaver to lightly tenderize the meat (Fig. 1). Cut the meat into bite-size pieces (Fig. 2). Mix with ① . Before deep-frying the meat, dredge it in 6 T. cornstarch (Fig. 3).

❷ Cut out the meaty part of the pineapple; retain the shell intact. Cut the pineapple into bite-size pieces (use only ½ c. pineapple). Separately cut the onion and bell pepper (seeds removed) into bitesize pieces. Separately mix ② together and ③ together.

❸ Heat the wok then add the oil for frying; deep-fry the meat over medium heat for 3 minutes; remove and reheat the oil until it is very hot (not smoking). Refry the meat for 30 seconds. Remove and drain. Remove the oil from the wok.

❹ Reheat the wok and add 1 T. oil. Stir-fry the bell pepper; add 1 T. water. Remove and drain. Add 3 T. oil; stir-fry garlic until fragrant. Add the onions and pineapple; stir-fry briefly then add ② . When the misture begins to boil add mixture ③ to thicken; stir. Add the fried meat and toss lightly; remove to pineapple shell and serve.

■ Pineapple may be substituted with one fresh tomato or bite-size pieces of carrot. If using fresh tomato, omit 2 T. pineapple juice and increase white vinegar to 3 T.

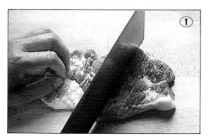

	2	lbs. brisket of beef	1	T. sugar
	3	T. cooking wine or sherry	2	c. water
①	6	T. soy sauce	½	c. beef stock (retained from
	2	green onions		steaming)
	2	slices of ginger root	1	1.7 oz. pkg. bean threads

❶ Place the beef in a pot of boiling water; boil and discard water. Add ① to the beef and cook. Turn the meat occasionally until all sides are cooked. Add the water; cover and cook over low heat for 1 hour or until tender. Add the sugar; cook for 10 minutes. Turn off the heat. Remove the meat and let it cool. Retain the liquid. Slice the meat after it has cooled.

❷ Soak the bean threads in water; after soaking, cut them in half. Place the bean threads in boiling water; bring to a boil. Remove and drain. Plunge the bean threads into cold water; drain.

❸ Arrange the sliced beef securely to line a medium-size heatproof bowl. Put the bean threads and beef stock in the center of the bowl. Steam over high heat for 20 minutes; remove. Place a pot holder under the bowl (Fig. 1). Put a plate, slightly larger than the bowl, over the bowl. Hold them together then tilt them slightly to drain the liquid. (Fig. 2). Invert the bowl on to a serving plate (Fig. 3). Remove the bowl and pour the retained liquid over the beef; serve.

Chop suey 炒雜碎 serves 6

	¼	lb. raw shrimp, shelled	1	T. green onion, ginger root, presoftened black mushrooms	shred-ded
①	dash of salt				
	1	t. cooking wine or sherry			
	1	t. cornstarch	⅓	c. shredded ham	
	¼	1b. lean meat: pork, beef, or chicken	1½	c. bean sprouts	
	1½	T. water	③ ¼	c. celery	shredded
②	1	t. cooking wine or sherry	½	c. carrot	
	dash of salt		½	T. cooking wine or sherry	
	1	t. cornstarch	4	T. water	
	½	c. oil	④ 1	t. cornstarch	mix
	1	oz. bean threads or rice noodles	½	t. salt, sugar	

❶ Cut the back of the shrimp lengthwise. Take a small mixture of water and salt solution to wash the shrimp; the dark vein should be removed. Rinse until the water is clear; drain. Mix the shrimp with ① ; add cornstarch, mix and marinate for 20 minutes.

❷ Shred the meat and add ②. Add cornstarch, mix, and marinate for 20 minutes. Fry the bean threads then put them in a serving platter.

❸ Heat the wok then add 3 T. oil. Put ③ in the wok; quickly stir-fry over high heat; drain and discard the oil.

❹ Heat the wok then add oil. When the oil is hot, separately stir-fry the shrimp then meat until the color changes (see p. 9 for precooking). Remove the meat; remove the oil from the wok. Reheat the wok. Add 2 T. oil. Stir-fry the onions, ginger root, and mushrooms until fragrant. Add the meat, shrimp, ③, cooking wine and ④ . Quickly stir-fry over high heat until thoroughly mixed; remove and put over the fried bean threads.

■ Method for deep-frying bean threads: Heat the wok then add 4 c. oil. When the oil is hot, put one bean thread in the oil. If the bean thread sinks to the bottom, the oil is not hot enough (Fig. 1). If the bean thread stays on the surface (Fig. 2) put remaining bean threads in the oil; quickly deep-fry (Fig. 3). Maintain appropriate heat to keep bean threads from burning. Remove and drain.

Skewered beef with sa tsa chang 沙茶牛肉串 serves 6

①
- ⅔ Ib. lean beef
- 1 T. soy sauce
- ½ T. cooking wine or sherry
- ½ T. water
- 1 T. cornstarch
- 1 T. oil

②
- 6 T. Sa Tsa Chang
- 1½ T. sugar
- 1 T. soy sauce
- 3 T. water
- 6 skewers

❶ Slice the beef into 1½-inch pieces. Add ① and mix well. Mix ② in a bowl for later use.

❷ Divide the sliced beef into 6 portions. Insert the sliced beef through the skewers.

❸ Heat the wok then add 1 T. oil. Add ② and bring it to a boil. Add the skewered beef and bring it to a boil again. Turn the skewered beef over. Cook for 1 minute over medium heat; remove and serve.

■ Sa Tsa Chang may be purchased at most Chinese markets.

■ Mix ② thoroughly before use; if the mixture is too thick, and water.

Sweet and sour pork 糖醋肉 serves 6

- ½ Ib. pork, beef, or chicken

①
- 1 egg yolk
- 1 T. cornstarch
- ½ T. soy sauce

- 6 T. cornstarch
- oil for frying
- ½ onion, pineapple
- 1 small bell pepper

- ½ t. chopped garlic
- 4 T. oil

②
- 3 T. sugar, water
- 2 T. pineapple juice, white vinegar
- 2 T. ketchup
- ½ t. salt

③
- 1 T. water
- 1½ t. cornstarch } mix

❶ Cut the meat into 2/3-inch slices. Use the blunt edge of a cleaver to lightly tenderize the meat (Fig. 1). Cut the meat into bite-size pieces (Fig. 2). Mix with ① . Before deep-frying the meat, dredge it in 6 T. cornstarch (Fig. 3).

❷ Cut out the meaty part of the pineapple; retain the shell intact. Cut the pineapple into bite-size pieces (use only ½ c. pineapple). Separately cut the onion and bell pepper (seeds removed) into bitesize pieces. Separately mix ② together and ③ together.

❸ Heat the wok then add the oil for frying; deep-fry the meat over medium heat for 3 minutes; remove and reheat the oil until it is very hot (not smoking). Refry the meat for 30 seconds. Remove and drain. Remove the oil from the wok.

❹ Reheat the wok and add 1 T. oil. Stir-fry the bell pepper; add 1 T. water. Remove and drain. Add 3 T. oil; stir-fry garlic until fragrant. Add the onions and pineapple; stir-fry briefly then add ② . When the misture begins to boil add mixture ③ to thicken; stir. Add the fried meat and toss lightly; remove to pineapple shell and serve.

■ Pineapple may be substituted with one fresh tomato or bite-size pieces of carrot. If using fresh tomato, omit 2 T. pineapple juice and increase white vinegar to 3 T.

①

②

③

紅燒牛肉(一)
Beef cooked in soy sauce   I
Bœuf sauce-soja

炒　雜　碎
Chop suey
Poulet sauté

洋葱牛肉
Stir-fried beef with onions
Bœuf à l'oignon

糯米丸子
Pearl balls
Boulettes de riz glutineux

41

Beef cooked in soy sauce I 紅燒牛肉（一） serves 6

	2	lbs. brisket of beef	
①	3	T. cooking wine or sherry	
	6	T. soy sauce	
	2	green onions	
	2	slices of ginger root	

1	T. sugar	
2	c. water	
½	c. beef stock (retained from steaming)	
1	1.7 oz. pkg. bean threads	

❶ Place the beef in a pot of boiling water; boil and discard water. Add ① to the beef and cook. Turn the meat occasionally until all sides are cooked. Add the water; cover and cook over low heat for 1 hour or until tender. Add the sugar; cook for 10 minutes. Turn off the heat. Remove the meat and let it cool. Retain the liquid. Slice the meat after it has cooled.

❷ Soak the bean threads in water; after soaking, cut them in half. Place the bean threads in boiling water; bring to a boil. Remove and drain. Plunge the bean threads into cold water; drain.

❸ Arrange the sliced beef securely to line a medium-size heatproof bowl. Put the bean threads and beef stock in the center of the bowl. Steam over high heat for 20 minutes; remove. Place a pot holder under the bowl (Fig. 1). Put a plate, slightly larger than the bowl, over the bowl. Hold them together then tilt them slightly to drain the liquid. (Fig. 2). Invert the bowl on to a serving plate (Fig. 3). Remove the bowl and pour the retained liquid over the beef; serve.

Chop suey 炒雜碎 serves 6

	¼	lb. raw shrimp, shelled
①	dash of salt	
	1	t. cooking wine or sherry
	1	t. cornstarch
	¼	1b. lean meat: pork, beef, or chicken
②	1½	T. water
	1	t. cooking wine or sherry
	dash of salt	
	1	t. cornstarch
	½	c. oil
	1	oz. bean threads or rice noodles

1	T. green onion, ginger root, presoftened black mushrooms	shredded	
③	⅓	c. shredded ham	
	1½	c. bean sprouts	
	¼	c. celery	shredded
	½	c. carrot	
	½	T. cooking wine or sherry	
④	4	T. water	
	1	t. cornstarch	mix
	½	t. salt, sugar	

❶ Cut the back of the shrimp lengthwise. Take a small mixture of water and salt solution to wash the shrimp; the dark vein should be removed. Rinse until the water is clear; drain. Mix the shrimp with ① ; add cornstarch, mix and marinate for 20 minutes.

❷ Shred the meat and add ② . Add cornstarch, mix, and marinate for 20 minutes. Fry the bean threads then put them in a serving platter.

❸ Heat the wok then add 3 T. oil. Put ③ in the wok; quickly stir-fry over high heat; drain and discard the oil.

❹ Heat the wok then add oil. When the oil is hot, separately stir-fry the shrimp then meat until the color changes (see p. 9 for precooking). Remove the meat; remove the oil from the wok. Reheat the wok. Add 2 T. oil. Stir-fry the onions, ginger root, and mushrooms until fragrant. Add the meat, shrimp, ③ , cooking wine and ④ . Quickly stir-fry over high heat until thoroughly mixed; remove and put over the fried bean threads.

■ Method for deep-frying bean threads: Heat the wok then add 4 c. oil. When the oil is hot, put one bean thread in the oil. If the bean thread sinks to the bottom, the oil is not hot enough (Fig. 1). If the bean thread stays on the surface (Fig. 2) put remaining bean threads in the oil; quickly deep-fry (Fig. 3). Maintain appropriate heat to keep bean threads from burning. Remove and drain.

Chicken legs cooked in soy sauce 紅燒鷄腿 serves 6

1⅓ lbs. chicken legs or chicken wings
1 T. soy sauce
oil for frying
1 potato
1 carrot
6 ½-inch pieces of green onion

1½ T. cooking wine or sherry

① { ½ T. sugar
4 T. soy sauce
1 c. water }

② { 1 T. water
2 t. cornstarch } mix

❶ Cut the chicken legs into bite-size pieces; add soy sauce and marinate for 20 minutes. Cut the potato and carrot into bite-size pieces, together to equal 2½cups.
❷ Heat the wok then add oil. Deep-fry the chicken for 3 minutes, or until golden; remove. Deep-fry the potatoes and carrots until they are golden; remove and drain. Remove the oil from the wok. Reheat the wok then add 1 T. oil. Stir-fry the onions. Add the chicken, wine, and ① ; bring them to a boil then turn the heat to low. Cover and cook for 5 minutes. Add the potatoes and carrots; cook for 10 minutes. The sauce will reduce to ½ cup. Slowly pour mixture ② while stirring gently. Remove and serve.
■ The potato is fried lightly golden to prevent its breaking apart during cooking.

Stir-fried chicken with vegetables 溜鷄片 serves 6

⅔ lb. chicken breasts
① { 3 T. water
¼ t. salt }
1 T. cornstarch
½ c. oil
6 ½-inch pieces of green onions
6 dried wood ears, presoftened
6 Chinese pea pods

½ celery rib

② { 1 c. water or stock
½ T. cooking wine or sherry
½ T. cornstarch
1 t. sugar
½ t. salt }
1 T. oil

❶ Remove the skin from the chicken and diagonally cut it into slices (Fig. 1). Mix the chicken with ① then add the cornstarch. Mix them together and let stand for 20 minutes. Remove the string from the pea pods (Fig. 2) then cut them diagonally in half. Slice the celery diagonally (Fig. 3).
❷ Heat the wok then add oil. Put the chicken in the wok when the oil is medium hot; stir-fry until the color changes. Remove and drain (see p. 9 for precooking). Remove the oil from the wok. Reheat the wok then put 1 T. oil in the wok. Stir-fry the onions; add ② and bring to a boil. Add the wood ears, pea pods, and celery. Bring to a boil again; add the chicken. Mix well; remove and serve.

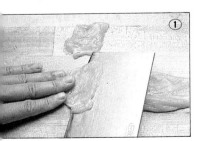
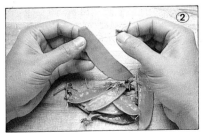

- ① {
  - ⅓   lb. pork loin, beef, or chicken
  - 1½   T. water
  - ½   T. soy sauce
  - 1   t. cooking wine or sherry
  }
- ½   T. cornstarch
- ¼   c. oil
- 3   eggs
- ⅓   lb. spinach
- 6   ½-inch pieces of green onion
- 6   slices of ginger root

- ② {
  - 1   c. precooked or canned bamboo shoot
  - ¼   c. presoftened wood ear
  - 2   T. presoftened black mushroom
  } shredded
- ½   T. cooking wine or sherry
- ③ {
  - 1½   T. soy sauce
  - ½   t. salt
  }
- 6   sheets of mandarin pancakes
- 3   T. hoisin sauce
- 9   T. oil

❶ Slice the pork and mix it with ① . Add the cornstarch and mix thoroughly. Marinate for 20 minutes. Beat the eggs. Mix ③ in a bowl. Cut the spinach into 3-inch pieces.

❷ Heat the wok then add 3 T. oil. Stir-fry the eggs until they solidify; remove. Add 3 T. oil and reheat the wok. Stir-fry the spinach; remove and drain.

❸ Heat the wok then add ¼ c. oil; stir-fry the meat until the color changes. Remove and drain (see p. 9 for precooking). Add 3 T. oil; stir-fry the ginger root and onions until fragrant. Add ② and stir-fry for 30 seconds. Add the meat, spinach, eggs and ③ . Turn the heat to high and toss lightly to mix; remove.

❹ Spread some hoisin sauce in the center of a mandarin pancake (Fig. 1). Place some moo-shu pork on top of the sauce (Fig. 2). Wrap the pancake into a roll (Fig. 3). Serve.

■ Frozen mandarin pancakes may be purchased at most Chinese markets. Allow the pancakes to thaw out before separating the sheets. Steam them for 4 minutes; remove and keep covered with a warm cloth to keep them moist.

Beef cooked in soy sauce II 紅燒牛肉(二) serves 6

- 2   lbs. brisket of beef.
- ① {
  - 2   green onions
  - 2   slices of ginger root
  - ½   c. soy sauce
  - 2   T. cooking wine or sherry
  - 2   c. water
  }

- 1   T. sugar
- 2   c. white radish, peeled thinly, cooked in water, and cut into bite-size pieces
- ② {
  - 1   T. water
  - 2   t. cornstarch
  } mix

● Cut the beef into bite-size pieces. Put them in a pot of boiling water; bring to a boil and discard water. Add ① ; cook, turning the meat occasionally, until all sides of the meat are cooked. Add water; cover and cook over low heat for 50 minutes, or until tender. Add sugar and cook for 10 minutes, or until the liquid is reduced to 2/3 cup. Add the precooked white radish then add mixture ② , to thicken; stir and serve.

■ Potatoes or carrots may be used instead of white radish.

Chicken legs cooked in soy sauce 紅燒鷄腿

1⅓	lbs. chicken legs or chicken wings		1½	T. cooking wine or sherry	
1	T. soy sauce		½	T. sugar	
	oil for frying	①	4	T. soy sauce	
1	potato		1	c. water	
1	carrot	②	1	T. water	mix
6	½-inch pieces of green onion		2	t. cornstarch	

❶ Cut the chicken legs into bite-size pieces; add soy sauce and marinate for 20 minutes. Cut the potato and carrot into bite-size pieces, together to equal 2½cups.

❷ Heat the wok then add oil. Deep-fry the chicken for 3 minutes, or until golden; remove. Deep-fry the potatoes and carrots until they are golden; remove and drain. Remove the oil from the wok. Reheat the wok then add 1 T. oil. Stir-fry the onions. Add the chicken, wine, and ① ; bring them to a boil then turn the heat to low. Cover and cook for 5 minutes. Add the potatoes and carrots; cook for 10 minutes. The sauce will reduce to ½ cup. Slowly pour mixture ② while stirring gently. Remove and serve.

■ The potato is fried lightly golden to prevent its breaking apart during cooking.

Stir-fried chicken with vegetables 溜鷄片

⅔	lb. chicken breasts		½	celery rib	
① 3	T. water		1	c. water or stock	
¼	t. salt		½	T. cooking wine or sherry	
1	T. cornstarch	②	½	T. cornstarch	
½	c. oil		1	t. sugar	
6	½-inch pieces of green onions		½	t. salt	
6	dried wood ears, presoftened		1	T. oil	
6	Chinese pea pods				

❶ Remove the skin from the chicken and diagonally cut it into slices (Fig. 1). Mix the chicken with ① then add the cornstarch. Mix them together and let stand for 20 minutes. Remove the string from the pea pods (Fig. 2) then cut them diagonally in half. Slice the celery diagonally (Fig. 3).

❷ Heat the wok then add oil. Put the chicken in the wok when the oil is medium hot; stir-fry until the color changes. Remove and drain (see p. 9 for precooking). Remove the oil from the wok. Reheat the wok then put 1 T. oil in the wok. Stir-fry the onions; add ② and bring to a boil. Add the wood ears, pea pods, and celery. Bring to a boil again; add the chicken. Mix well; remove and serve.

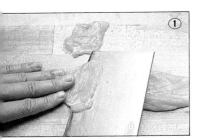

木須肉
Moo-shu pork
Porc Moo-shu

紅燒牛肉(二)
Beef cooked in soy sauce
Bœuf sauce soja

II

48

炸 生 蠔
Deep-fried oysters
Beignets d'huîtres

魚 香 鮮 貝
Spicy scallops
Escalopes épicées

49

Moo-shu pork 木須肉 serves 6

<table>
<tr><td>

⅓ lb. pork loin, beef, or chicken

① { 1½ T. water
½ T. soy sauce
1 t. cooking wine or sherry

½ T. cornstarch
¼ c. oil
3 eggs
⅓ lb. spinach
6 ½-inch pieces of green onion
6 slices of ginger root

</td><td>

② { 1 c. precooked or canned bamboo shoot
¼ c. presoftened wood ear
2 T. presoftened black mushroom } shredded

½ T. cooking wine or sherry
③ { 1½ T. soy sauce
½ t. salt

6 sheets of mandarin pancakes
3 T. hoisin sauce
9 T. oil

</td></tr>
</table>

❶ Slice the pork and mix it with ① . Add the cornstarch and mix thoroughly. Marinate for 20 minutes. Beat the eggs. Mix ③ in a bowl. Cut the spinach into 3-inch pieces.

❷ Heat the wok then add 3 T. oil. Stir-fry the eggs until they solidify; remove. Add 3 T. oil and reheat the wok. Stir-fry the spinach; remove and drain.

❸ Heat the wok then add ¼ c. oil; stir-fry the meat until the color changes. Remove and drain (see p. 9 for precooking). Add 3 T. oil; stir-fry the ginger root and onions until fragrant. Add ② and stir-fry for 30 seconds. Add the meat, spinach, eggs and ③ . Turn the heat to high and toss lightly to mix; remove.

❹ Spread some hoisin sauce in the center of a mandarin pancake (Fig. 1). Place some moo-shu pork on top of the sauce (Fig. 2). Wrap the pancake into a roll (Fig. 3). Serve.

■ Frozen mandarin pancakes may be purchased at most Chinese markets. Allow the pancakes to thaw out before separating the sheets. Steam them for 4 minutes; remove and keep covered with a warm cloth to keep them moist.

Beef cooked in soy sauce II 紅燒牛肉（二） serves 6

<table>
<tr><td>

2 lbs. brisket of beef.

① { 2 green onions
2 slices of ginger root
½ c. soy sauce
2 T. cooking wine or sherry
2 c. water

</td><td>

1 T. sugar
2 c. white radish, peeled thinly, cooked in water, and cut into bite-size pieces

② { 1 T. water
2 t. cornstarch } mix

</td></tr>
</table>

● Cut the beef into bite-size pieces. Put them in a pot of boiling water; bring to a boil and discard water. Add ① ; cook, turning the meat occasionally, until all sides of the meat are cooked. Add water; cover and cook over low heat for 50 minutes, or until tender. Add sugar and cook for 10 minutes, or until the liquid is reduced to 2/3 cup. Add the precooked white radish then add mixture ② , to thicken; stir and serve.

■ Potatoes or carrots may be used instead of white radish.

Deep-fried oysters 炸生蠔

6 fresh oysters (about 2/3 lb.)

① ⎰ 1 T. cooking wine or sherry
   ⎨ 2 green onions
   ⎱ 2 slices of ginger root

② ⎰ ½ T. flour
   ⎱ ¼ t. salt

½ c. flour
1 egg, lightly beaten
1 c. bread crumbs
oil for frying

❶ Wash the oysters in salt water and rinse in clear water; drain. Add ① and marinate for 20 minutes. Place ② in a bowl and mix.

❷ Coat the oysters with the flour (Fig. 1) then dip them in the lightly beaten egg (Fig. 2). Coat the oysters with bread crumbs (Fig. 3).

❸ Heat the wok then add the oil. Deep-fry the oysters for 3 minutes, or until they are cooked thoroughly and the outside is crispy. Remove and drain.

■ Serve with Szechuan peppercorn salt or ketchup.

Spicy scallops 魚香鮮貝

12 fresh scallops (about 1 lb.)

① ⎰ 1 T. cooking wine or sherry
   ⎨ 1 green onion
   ⎱ 2 slices of ginger root

② ⎰ 4 T. cornstarch ⎰
   ⎨ 2 T. water ⎬ mix
   ⎱ 1 egg white ⎱

3 T. flour
oil for frying

③ ⎰ 2 T. green onions ⎰
   ⎨ 1 T. ginger root ⎬ chopped
   ⎨ ½ T. garlice ⎪
   ⎱ 1 t. hot chili paste ⎱

④ ⎰ 4 T. water ⎰
   ⎨ 1 t. sugar ⎪
   ⎨ ½ t. salt ⎪
   ⎨ ½ t. cornstarch ⎬ mix
   ⎨ 1 t. cooking wine or sherry ⎪
   ⎱ 1 t. white vinegar ⎱

2 T. oil

❶ Wash the scallops and marinate them in ① for 20 minutes. Mix the water and cornstarch from ② then add the egg white (cornstarch mixture).

❷ Heat the wok then add oil. Coat the scallops with flour then dip them in the cornstarch mixture. Deep-fry the scallops for 3 minutes; remove to a serving dish.

❸ Heat the wok then add 2 T. oil; stir-fry ③ until fragrant. Add ④; bring to a boil then pour over the scallops. Serve.

Steamed crab 清蒸蟹 serves 6

① {
1 medium-size crab
1 T. cooking wine or sherry
2 green onions
2 slices of ginger root
}

Dipping Sauce:

② {
1 T. chopped ginger root
2 T. white vinegar
¼ t. salt
}

or

③ {
½ T. chopped garlic clove
½ T. cooking wine or sherry
2 T. soy sauce
}

❶ To clean the crab: Hold it upside down; use a sharp-pointed knife or chopstick to pierce the shell through the center until it stops moving. Remove the knife. Hold the crab by the legs and remove the upper shell. Remove the spongy gills and lightly rinse the inside with cold water; a soft brush may be used to remove any dirt and runny matter.

❷ Place the crab in pan; put ① on top of the crab and steam over high heat for 10 minutes. When the crab is cooked, cut it into bite-size pieces. Serve hot; use ② or ③ as dipping sauce.

Fish cooked in soy sauce 紅燒魚 serves 12

① {
1 yellow fish (about 1⅔ lbs.)
1 T. cooking wine or sherry
1 t. salt
}
2 green onions, cut into 8 pieces
3 presoftened black mushrooms, cut into bite-size pieces
12 slices lean meat; pork, beef, or chicken

12 slices bamboo shoot
1 T. cooking wine or sherry

② {
1 c. stock or water
1 T. sugar
4 T. soy sauce
}

③ {
½ T. cornstarch
1 T. water
} mix
4 T. oil

❶ Scale and clean the fish, if necessary; drain. Mix with ① . Before frying, pat dry.

❷ Heat the wok then add 4 T. oil. Swirl the oil in the wok to cover the lower two-thirds of the wok. Hold the fish by the tail; place it on the edge of the wok. Gradually lower the fish into the wok. Fry the whole fish completely on one side then turn it to completely fry the fish until golden; move aside or remove from the wok.

❸ Add oil if needed. Stir-fry the onions until fragrant; add the mushrooms and lightly stir-fry. Add the meat and bamboo shoots and stir-fry. Return the fish to the center of the wok and add wine and ② . Cover and bring to a boil; cook over medium heat for 8 minutes, or until the liquid is reduced to about ½ cup. Transfer the fish to a serving platter. Add mixture ③ to the liquid in the wok; stir then pour over the fish. Serve.

■ Sea bass, perch, or carp may be substituted; however, carp may be too boney for this dish.

Stir-fried fish with fermented soy beans 豉汁魚球 serves 6

① {
⅔ lb. fish meat, fillet or steak
½ T. cooking wine or sherry
⅔ t. salt
}
1 T. cornstarch
½ c. oil
½ c. onions, cut into bite-size pieces
2 T. oil

② {
1 T. ginger root
½ T. garlic clove
} chopped
1 T. fermented soy beans
½ c. bell pepper, cut into bite-size pieces

⅓ t. cooking wine or sherry

③ {
4 T. water
1 t. cornstarch
½ t. sugar
⅓ t. salt
}

❶ Score the fillets lightly in criss cross fashion; then cut them into bite-size pieces. Mix with ① and cornstarch; marinate for 20 minutes.

❷ Heat the wok then add oil. When the oil is hot put the fish in the wok. Stir-fry until the color changes; remove and drain. Remove the oil from the wok (see p. 9 for precooking). Add 2 T. oil; stir-fry the onions and ② until they are fragrant. Add the pepper, fish, wine, and ③ ; toss lightly. Remove to a serving platter.

■ Fermented soy beans may be purchased at most Chinese markets.

54

Deep-fried oysters 炸生蠔 serves 6

	6	fresh oysters (about 2/3 lb.)
①	1	T. cooking wine or sherry
	2	green onions
	2	slices of ginger root

②	½	T. flour
	¼	t. salt
	½	c. flour
	1	egg, lightly beaten
	1	c. bread crumbs
		oil for frying

❶ Wash the oysters in salt water and rinse in clear water; drain. Add ① and marinate for 20 minutes. Place ② in a bowl and mix.

❷ Coat the oysters with the flour (Fig. 1) then dip them in the lightly beaten egg (Fig. 2). Coat the oysters with bread crumbs (Fig. 3).

❸ Heat the wok then add the oil. Deep-fry the oysters for 3 minutes, or until they are cooked thoroughly and the outside is crispy. Remove and drain.

■ Serve with Szechuan peppercorn salt or ketchup.

Spicy scallops 魚香鮮貝 serves 6

	12	fresh scallops (about 1 lb.)
①	1	T. cooking wine or sherry
	1	green onion
	2	slices of ginger root
②	4	T. cornstarch
	2	T. water
	1	egg white

mix

	3	T. flour
		oil for frying
③	2	T. green onions
	1	T. ginger root
	½	T. garlice
	1	t. hot chili paste

chopped

	4	T. water
④	1	t. sugar
	½	t. salt
	½	t. cornstarch
	1	t. cooking wine or sherry
	1	t. white vinegar
	2	T. oil

mix

❶ Wash the scallops and marinate them in ① for 20 minutes. Mix the water and cornstarch from ② then add the egg white (cornstarch mixture).

❷ Heat the wok then add oil. Coat the scallops with flour then dip them in the cornstarch mixture. Deep-fry the scallops for 3 minutes; remove to a serving dish.

❸ Heat the wok then add 2 T. oil; stir-fry ③ until fragrant. Add ④; bring to a boil then pour over the scallops. Serve.

51

清　蒸　蟹
Steamed crab
Crabe à l'étuvée

紅　燒　魚
Fish cooked in soy sauce
Poisson sauce soja

豉汁魚球
Stir-fried fish with fermented soy beans
Filets de poisson aux haricots noirs férmenté

瓦 塊 魚 片
Spicy fish fillet
Filets de poisson sauce épicée

青 蒸 魚
Steamed fish
Poisson à l'étuvée

53

Steamed crab 清蒸蟹 serves 6

1 medium-size crab

① {
1 T. cooking wine or sherry
2 green onions
2 slices of ginger root
}

Dipping Sauce:

② {
1 T. chopped ginger root
2 T. white vinegar
¼ t. salt
}

or

③ {
½ T. chopped garlic clove
½ T. cooking wine or sherry
2 T. soy sauce
}

❶ To clean the crab: Hold it upside down; use a sharp-pointed knife or chopstick to pierce the shell through the center until it stops moving. Remove the knife. Hold the crab by the legs and remove the upper shell. Remove the spongy gills and lightly rinse the inside with cold water; a soft brush may be used to remove any dirt and runny matter.

❷ Place the crab in pan; put ① on top of the crab and steam over high heat for 10 minutes. When the crab is cooked, cut it into bite-size pieces. Serve hot; use ② or ③ as dipping sauce.

Fish cooked in soy sauce 紅燒魚 serves 12

1 yellow fish (about 1⅔ lbs.)

① {
1 T. cooking wine or sherry
1 t. salt
}

2 green onions, cut into 8 pieces
3 presoftened black mushrooms, cut into bite-size pieces
12 slices lean meat; pork, beef, or chicken

12 slices bamboo shoot
1 T. cooking wine or sherry

② {
1 c. stock or water
1 T. sugar
4 T. soy sauce
}

③ {
½ T. cornstarch
1 T. water
} mix

4 T. oil

❶ Scale and clean the fish, if necessary; drain. Mix with ① . Before frying, pat dry.

❷ Heat the wok then add 4 T. oil. Swirl the oil in the wok to cover the lower two-thirds of the wok. Hold the fish by the tail; place it on the edge of the wok. Gradually lower the fish into the wok. Fry the whole fish completely on one side then turn it to completely fry the fish until golden; move aside or remove from the wok.

❸ Add oil if needed. Stir-fry the onions until fragrant; add the mushrooms and lightly stir-fry. Add the meat and bamboo shoots and stir-fry. Return the fish to the center of the wok and add wine and ② . Cover and bring to a boil; cook over medium heat for 8 minutes, or until the liquid is reduced to about ½ cup. Transfer the fish to a serving platter. Add mixture ③ to the liquid in the wok; stir then pour over the fish. Serve.

■ Sea bass, perch, or carp may be substituted; however, carp may be too boney for this dish.

Stir-fried fish with fermented soy beans 豉汁魚球 serves 6

① {
⅔ lb. fish meat, fillet or steak
½ T. cooking wine or sherry
⅔ t. salt
}

1 T. cornstarch
½ c. oil
½ c. onions, cut into bite-size pieces
2 T. oil

② {
1 T. ginger root
½ T. garlic clove
} chopped

1 T. fermented soy beans
½ c. bell pepper, cut into bite-size pieces

⅓ t. cooking wine or sherry

③ {
4 T. water
1 t. cornstarch
½ t. sugar
⅓ t. salt
}

❶ Score the fillets lightly in criss cross fashion; then cut them into bite-size pieces. Mix with ① and cornstarch; marinate for 20 minutes.

❷ Heat the wok then add oil. When the oil is hot put the fish in the wok. Stir-fry until the color changes; remove and drain. Remove the oil from the wok (see p. 9 for precooking). Add 2 T. oil; stir-fry the onions and ② until they are fragrant. Add the pepper, fish, wine, and ③ ; toss lightly.. Remove to a serving platter.

■ Fermented soy beans may be purchased at most Chinese markets.

Spicy fish fillet 瓦塊魚片 serves 6

⅔ lb. fish meat: fillet or steak

① { ½ T. cooking wine or sherry
    ⅓ t. salt

② { 1 egg
    4 T. cornstarch, flour
    3 T. water

oil for frying

③ { 1½ T. green onions
    1 T. ginger root
    ½ T. garlic clove } chopped

④ { 1 T. cooking wine or sherry
    3 T. ketchup
    1 t. hot chili paste

⑤ { ¾ c. water
    1 T. sugar
    ½ T. cornstarch
    ¾ t. salt
    2 T. oil

❶ If the fish meat is thick, slice it lengthwise. Cut the fish meat into small steaks or fillets (Fig. 1). Add ① ; marinate for 20 minutes. Mix ② together (coating).

❷ Heat the wok then add oil. Dredge the fish steaks in the coating (Fig. 2). Deep-fry the fish over medium heat for 3 minutes or until the fish is thoroughly cooked and the outside is crispy (Fig. 3). Remove to a serving platter. Remove the oil from the wok.

❸ Reheat the wok then add 2 T. oil. Stir-fry ③ until fragrant; add ④ and stir-fry. Add ⑤ ; bring to a boil then pour over the fish. Serve.

Steamed fish 清蒸魚 serves 6

① { 1 fish (perch), (about 1 lb.)
    1 T. cooking wine or sherry
    1 t. salt
    2 green onions
    2 slices of ginger root

② { dash of pepper
    ½ t. sesame oil
    2 T. shredded green onion
    2 T. oil

❶ Marinate the fish with ① ; place two chopsticks on a heatproof plate to form a rack for the fish. Lay the fish on the chopsticks. Put the plate in a steamer and steam for minutes, or until cooked.

❷ Remove the fish and the liquid to a serving platter. Sprinkle ② and the green onions on top of the fish. Drizzle 2 T. hot oil over the fish and serve.

乾燒蝦仁
Shrimp with ketchup
Crevettes sautées sauce tomate

三 色 蝦
Shrimp with vegetables
Crevettes trois couleurs

醋 辣 蝦
Sour and hot shrimp
Crevettes à la sauce aigre-douce

芙 蓉 蝦
Shrimp foo yung
Crevettes Foo-yung

57

Shrimp with ketchup 乾燒蝦仁 serves 6

① {
- ⅔ lb. shrimp, shelled
- 1 egg white
- 1½ T. cornstarch
- 2 T. water
- 1 T. oil
- ½ T. cooking wine or sherry
- ½ t. salt
- ½ c. oil
}

② {
- ½ c. chopped onion
- ½ T. chopped ginger root
- ½ T. chopped garlic clove
}

③ {
- 1 T. cooking wine or sherry
- 3 T. ketchup
- 1 T. hot chili paste
}

④ {
- 1 T. sugar
- 5 T. water
- 1 t. cornstarch
- ½ t. salt
} mix
- 2 T. precooked green peas or chopped green onion
- 3 T. oil

❶ Use a cleaver to cut the back of the shrimp lengthwise. Remove the dark vein (Fig. 1). Put 1 t. salt and 1 T. water on the shrimp and gently work the salt-water solution into the shrimp (Fig. 2). Rinse the shrimp (Fig. 3). Continue rinsing until the water is clear; drain. Add the wine and salt from ① ; mix. Add the water and mix. Let stand for 5 minutes. Add the egg white (p. 59, fig. 4) and mix. Add the cornstarch (p. 59, fig. 5); mix. Add the oil (p. 59, fig. 6); mix.

❷ Place ingredients of ②, ③, and mixture ④ in separate bowls.

❸ Heat the wok then add the oil. When the oil is hot put the shrimp in the wok. Stir-fry the shrimp until the color changes; remove and drain (see p. 9 for precooking). Remove the oil from the wok. Reheat the wok then add 3 T. oil. Stir-fry ② until they are fragrant. Add ③ . Continue to stir-fry; add ④ . Bring to a boil; add the shrimp and green peas. Quickly stir-fry until thoroughly mixed; remove and serve.

■ If whole shrimp are used, omit water in ① .

Shrimp with vegetables 三色蝦 serves 6

- ⅔ lb. shrimp, shelled
- ① same as for Shrimp with ketchup (shown above)
- ½ c. oil
- ½ stem of broccoli, cut lengthwise then sliced into 6 paper-thin slices)
- ½ tomato, cut across into 6 slices
- 1 green onion, cut into 6 pieces

② {
- 1 T. cooking wine or sherry
- 1 T. water
- ⅓ t. cornstarch
- ¼ t. salt
}

❶ Follow directions given in step 1, p. 58 Shrimp with ketchup, pp. 58-59, figures 1-6.

❷ Heat the wok then add the oil. When the oil is hot put the shrimp in the wok. Stir-fry the shrimp until the color changes; remove and drain (see p. 9 for precooking). Remove the oil from the wok. Reheat the wok then add 3 T. oil. Stir-fry the onions until they are fragrant. Add the sliced broccoli and tomato; stir-fry. Add the shrimp and ② . Heat over high heat and quickly stir-fry until the ingredients are completely mixed; remove and serve.

■ If whole shrimp are used, omit water in ① .

Sour and hot shrimp 醋辣蝦

⅓ lb. shrimp, shelled
① same as for Shrimp with ketchup, p. 58
½ c. cornstarch
oil for frying

② {
2 T. chopped green onions
½ T. ginger root
½ T. garlic clove
} chopped
1 t. hot chili paste

③ {
1½ T. sugar
2 T. soy sauce, water
1 T. white vinegar
1 t. sesame oil
2 T. oil

❶ Follow directions given in step 1, p. 58 Shrimp with ketchup, pp. 58-59, figures 1-6.
❷ Add ½ c. cornstarch to the shrimp and mix them.
❸ Heat the wok then add the oil for frying. When the oil is hot, deep-fry the shrimp over medium heat for 1½ minutes, or until the outside is crispy; drain and remove. Remove the oil from the wok.
❹ Reheat the wok then add 2 T. oil. Stir-fry ② until ingredients are fragrant; add ③ . Bring to a boil then add the shrimp, sesame oil; mix. Remove and serve.
■ Hot chili paste may be purchased at most Chinese markets.
■ The soy sauce may be substituted with ketchup and a dash of salt.
■ If whole shrimp are used, omit water in ① .

Shrimp foo yung 芙蓉蝦

serves 6

4 oz. shrimp, shelled
① {
1 T. water
½ T. oil
¼ t. salt
2 t. cornstarch
1 t. cooking wine or sherry
½ egg white
½ c. oil for frying

② {
6 egg whites
dash of salt
½ t. cornstarch
1 t. water
1 t. cooking wine or sherry

oil for frying
2 slices ham
3 large button mushrooms
½ stem of broccoli, cut lengthwise then sliced into 6 paper-thin slices, OR
6 paper-thin slices of cucumber

③ {
½ c. water
1 t. cornstarch
1 t. cooking wine or sherry
¼ t. salt
} mix

❶ Follow directions given in step 1, p. 58 Shrimp with ketchup, pp. 58-59, figures 1-6.
❷ Cut the sliced ham into ½-inch diamond shapes. Slice the button mushrooms.
❸ Heat the wok then add ½ c. oil. Stir-fry the shrimp until the color changes; drain (see p. 9 for precooking).
❹ Reheat the wok then add the oil for frying. When the oil is hot, deep-fry ② over medium heat until it rises to the surface. Add the ham, mushrooms, slices of broccoli (to warm them); remove and drain. Remove the oil from the wok. Put mixture ③ in the wok and bring to a boil. Add all the deep-fried ingredients; stir. Remove and serve.
■ Sandwich ham may be used.
■ If whole shrimp are used, omit water in ① .

軟酥明蝦
Jumbo shrimp with ketchup
Super crevettes à la sauce tomate

清炒蝦仁
Stir-fried shrimp
Crevettes sautées et brocoli

素 菜 捲
Vegetable rolls
Rouleaux de printemps aux légumes

油 泡 蝦
Shrimp with soy sauce
Crevettes sauce soja

61

Jumbo shrimp with ketchup 軟酥明蝦 serves 6

6 jumbo shrimp, (about ½ lb.)	
① { 1 t. cooking wine or sherry ⅛ t. salt ½ egg white 1 T. cornstarch	③ { 1½ T. sugar 1 T. cooking wine or sherry 1 T. white vinegar 3 T. ketchup 3 T. water ½ t. salt 1 t. cornstarch } mix 2 T. oil
② { ⅔ c. (3 oz.) powdered glutinous rice 6½ T. water ½ t. baking powder	
oil for frying	

❶ Shell the shrimp and leave the tail intact (Fig. 1). Wash the shrimp in a salt-water solution and rinse thoroughly in clear water; drain. Use a cleaver to cut the back of the shrimp in half lengthwise (Fig. 2) but do not break apart. Remove the dark vein. With the tip of the cleaver, make a slit lengthwise in the center of each half of shrimp (Fig. 3). Use the lower tip of the blade to prick each half of the shrimp several times so that it will not curl while frying. Mix with ① and add 1 T. cornstarch. Marinate for 20 minutes. Mix ② to form a paste. Place ③ in a separate bowl.

❷ Heat the wok then add the oil for frying. Turn the heat to medium. *Hold the shrimp by the tail and dip it into paste ② then put it in the wok*. Repeat from * for the remaining shrimp. Deep-fry the shrimp for 5 minutes then remove. Reheat the oil and refry the shrimp for 20 seconds. This procedure will make the shrimp crispy outside and tender inside. Drain. Remove the oil. Reheat the wok then add 2 T. oil. Add ③ ; bring to a boil and add the shrimp; stir-fry until ingredients are completely mixed. serve .

Stir-fried shrimp 清炒蝦仁 serves 6

⅔ lb. shrimp, shelled	
① { 1 egg white 1½ T. cornstarch 2 T. water ½ T. cooking wine or sherry 1 T. oil ½ t. salt ½ c. oil	② { 1 T. water 1 T. cooking wine or sherry 1 t. cornstarch ⅓ t. salt } mix 1 t. sesame oil 8 flowerets of broccoli

❶ Follow directions given in step 1, p. 58 Shrimp with ketchup, pp. 58-59, figures 1-6.

❷ Boil water and cook the broccoli; remove.

❸ Heat the wok then add the oil. When the oil is hot put the shrimp in the wok. Stir-fry the shrimp until the color changes; remove and drain (see p. 9 for precooking). Remove the oil from the wok. Reheat the wok then add 1 T. oil. Add ② and the shrimp; stir to mix. Sprinkle the sesame oil over the shrimp then transfer them to a serving plate. Garnish with the broccoli flowerets; serve.

■ If whole shrimp are used, omit water in ① .

62

Vegetable rolls 素菜捲 serves 6

6 leaves of cabbage	1 T. shredded ginger root
½ lb. white radish	2 oz. carrots
① { ½ T. white vinegar, sugar dash of pepper 1 t. sesame oil	2 hot red peppers 2 T. presoftened, chopped wood ears

❶ Rinse the cabbage. Use a sharp knife to cut into and around the core of the cabbage (Fig. 1). Place the whole cabbage in boiling water. Use chopsticks to separate the leaves from the core (Fig. 2). Remove and plunge them into cold water; drain thoroughly. Cut out the length of the stems (Fig. 3).

❷ Peel the white radish and shred it. Add 1 t. salt to soften the radish; let it stand for 10 minutes then drain. Squeeze out excess water. Add ① and the ginger root; mix thoroughly.

❸ Peel and shred the carrot; add a little salt to soften it. Slice the peppers.

❹ Place two slices of pepper, a portion of white radish and carrot in the middle of each half of cabbage leaf. Wrap filling like an egg roll. Cut each roll in half. Sprinkle chopped wood ear on the open ends. Place the rolls on a serving plate and serve.

Shrimp with soy sauce 油泡蝦 serves 6

⅔ lb. shrimp, with shell	oil for frying
① { 1½ T. sugar ½ T. green onion } chopped ½ T. ginger root 2 T. soy sauce 1 T. cooking wine or sherry 1 t. cornstarch	1 t. sesame oil

❶ Use scissors to cut the back of the shrimp lengthwise; remove the dark vein. Wash in salt and water solution and rinse in clear water.

❷ Heat the wok then add the oil. Deep-fry the shrimp until the color changes; remove and drain. Remove the oil from the wok. Put 1 T. oil in the wok; add ① then add the shrimp. Quickly stir-fry until the ingredients are thoroughly mixed. Add 1 t. sesame oil; remove and serve.

拌 黄 瓜
Spicy cucumber salad
Concombres en salade

四川泡菜
Szechuan-style pickled salad
Salade à la mode du Szechuan

廣東泡菜
Cantonese pickled vegetables
Salade à la mode cantonnaise

醋拌三絲
Carrot, cucumber, and Chinese radish salad
Salade trois couleurs

涼拌白蘿蔔
Chinese radish salad
Navets en salade

辣白菜
Pickled Chinese cabbage
Salade de chou épicé

拌高麗菜
Pickled cabbage
Chou mariné

泡黃瓜片
Cucumber salad
Concombre mariné

Spicy cucumber salad 拌黄瓜 serves 6

1⅓ lbs. cucumber
1   T. salt

① { 1 T. chopped garlic, sesame oil
    1 t. sugar, white vinegar, hot chili paste }

❶ Cut off the ends of the cucumbers. Cut the cucumbers into bite-size pieces. Add salt; mix and let stand for 1 hour.
❷ Lightly rinse the cucumber; drain. Add ① and mix. Refrigerate for 6 hours; serve.

Carrot, cucumber, and white radish salad 醋拌三絲

serves 6

① { 1   c. white radish
    ½   c. carrot
    ½   c. cucumber } pared and shredded
    1   t. salt

② { 1   T. white vinegar
    1   t. sugar
    ½   t. sesame oil }

❶ Combine ① and add the salt. Let stand for 1 hour.
❷ Lightly rinse the vegetables; drain. Add ②, mix then serve.

White radish salad 涼拌白蘿蔔 serves 6

1   lb. white radishes (daikon)
1   t. salt
¼   c. chopped coriander

① { 1 T. white vinegar
    1 t. sugar, sesame oil
    1 T. soy sauce }

❶ Pare and shred the radishes. Add salt and let stand for 1 hour.
❷ Rinse the radishes in clear water and drain. Add ① and coriander; mix. Sprinkle soy sauce on radish then toss lightly before serving.
■ The salad will keep for two or three days if refrigerated.

Szechuan-style pickled salad 四川泡菜 serves 6

nappa cabbage
white radish } combined to equal 2 lbs.
carrot
2   hot red peppers, cut into ½-inch pieces

① { 6 c. purified water
    3 T. salt
    2 T. cooking wine or sherry
    1 t. Szechuan peppercorn }

❶ Rinse the cabbage and tear it into 2-inch pieces. Rinse the carrot and radish; dice and drain them thoroughly. Allow the vegetables to dry for one-half day.
❷ Place ① in a sterilized glass jar; add the vegetables. The vegetables should be completely covered by ①. Cover the jar tightly with an air-tight lid. The pickled salad will be ready to eat in 3-4 days.
■ 1. When removing vegetables from the marinade, use sterilized utensil or chopsticks to prevent any foreign matter from getting into the marinade.
  2. The marinade may be used several times and will improve with age. If necessary, add more of ① so that the vegetables are always covered while marinating.
  3. The vegetables may be cut into different sizes and shapes.

Cantonese pickled vegetables 廣東泡菜 serves 6

① { ½ white radish }
  { ½ carrot } cut into bite-size pieces to equal 2 cups (about 2/3 lb.)
  { 1 cucumber }
  ½ T. salt

② { 3 T. sugar
    3 T. white vinegar }

❶ Add the salt to ① and let stand for 6 hours.
❷ Lightly rinse and drain the vegetables. Add ② ; mix and let stand in the refrigerator for 6 hours. Serve. (The vegetables will taste better if pickled for 1 or 2 days.)
■ Ingredients in ① may be diced, shredded, or diagonally cross-cut into bite-size pieces, or smaller pieces if desired. The marinating time should be revised accordingly. Smaller pieces should be pickled for a shorter time. Slices of ginger root and hot red pepper may be used.

Pickled nappa cabbage 辣白菜 serves 6

1 lb. nappa cabbage
⅔ T. salt

① { 1½ T. hot chili powder
    1 t. chopped garlic clove
    1 t. juice extracted from ginger root
    1 t. white vinegar }

❶ Wash and drain the cabbage. Dry thoroughly dry with a paper towel. Tear the cabbage into bite-size pieces. Sprinkle the salt over the cabbage and let stand for 2 hours. Drain; squeeze out excess water. Mix with ① .
❷ Put the cabbage in a sterilized jar; cover with an air-tight lid. The cabbage will be ready to eat within 2 or 3 days.
■ When removing cabbage from marinade, use sterilized utensils or clean chopsticks to prevent any foreign matter from getting into the marinade.

Pickled cabbage 拌高麗菜 serves 6

1 lb. cabbage
2 t. salt
½ t. salt

❶ Wash, drain, and shred the cabbage. Mix the cabbage and 2 t. salt in a bowl. Let stand for 1 hour.
❷ Lightly wash and drain the cabbage. Add ½ t. salt and mix. Sprinkle soy sauce on the cabbage before eating.
■ When removing any pickled vegetables from marinate, use clean chopsticks to prevent any foreign matter from getting into the marinade.

Cucumber salad 泡黃瓜片 serves 6

1 c. sliced cucumber

① { 1 c. water
    1 t. salt }

● Slice the cucumber and soak it in ① for 10 minutes; drain and serve.
■ The cucumbers may be rinsed if they are too salty. Season with other spices.

Stir-fried spinach 炒菠菜

1⅓ lb. spinach

①{ 1 T. chopped garlic
2 T. water
1 t. salt
2 T. oil

❶ Wash the spinach and tear it into pieces 2 inches long.
❷ Heat the wok then add 2 T. oil. Stir-fry the spinach over high heat and add ① . Quickly stir-fry until thoroughly mixed. Serve.

Stir-fried cabbage 炒高麗菜

⅔ lb. cabbage
1 medium-size tomato
2 T. oil

①{ 3 T. water
2 t. sugar
⅔ t. salt

❶ Cut the cabbage and tomato into bite-size pieces.
❷ Heat the wok then add 2 T. oil. Stir-fry the tomato lightly then add the cabbage; add ① Quickly stir-fry until thoroughly mixed. Serve.

Stir-fried bean sprouts 炒豆芽菜

⅔ lb. bean sprouts
2 T. oil
⅔ t. salt

● Wash the bean sprouts. Heat the wok then add 2 T. oil. Stir-fry the bean sprouts over high heat then add the salt. Quickly stir-fry the bean sprouts until thoroughly mixed. Serve.
■ If preparing this dish for guests, both ends of the bean sprouts may be removed. Use stems only.

Cantonese pickled vegetables 廣東泡菜 serves 6

① {
½ white radish
½ carrot
1 cucumber
} cut into bite-size pieces to equal 2 cups (about 2/3 lb.)
½ T. salt

② {
3 T. sugar
3 T. white vinegar
}

❶ Add the salt to ① and let stand for 6 hours.
❷ Lightly rinse and drain the vegetables. Add ② ; mix and let stand in the refrigerator for 6 hours. Serve. (The vegetables will taste better if pickled for 1 or 2 days.)
■ Ingredients in ① may be diced, shredded, or diagonally cross-cut into bite-size pieces, or smaller pieces if desired. The marinating time should be revised accordingly. Smaller pieces should be pickled for a shorter time. Slices of ginger root and hot red pepper may be used.

Pickled nappa cabbage 辣白菜 serves 6

1 lb. nappa cabbage
⅔ T. salt

① {
1½ T. hot chili powder
1 t. chopped garlic clove
1 t. juice extracted from ginger root
1 t. white vinegar
}

❶ Wash and drain the cabbage. Dry thoroughly dry with a paper towel. Tear the cabbage into bite-size pieces. Sprinkle the salt over the cabbage and let stand for 2 hours. Drain; squeeze out excess water. Mix with ① .
❷ Put the cabbage in a sterilized jar; cover with an air-tight lid. The cabbage will be ready to eat within 2 or 3 days.
■ When removing cabbage from marinade, use sterilized utensils or clean chopsticks to prevent any foreign matter from getting into the marinade.

Pickled cabbage 拌高麗菜 serves 6

1 lb. cabbage
2 t. salt
½ t. salt

❶ Wash, drain, and shred the cabbage. Mix the cabbage and 2 t. salt in a bowl. Let stand for 1 hour.
❷ Lightly wash and drain the cabbage. Add ½ t. salt and mix. Sprinkle soy sauce on the cabbage before eating.
■ When removing any pickled vegetables from marinate, use clean chopsticks to prevent any foreign matter from getting into the marinade.

Cucumber salad 泡黃瓜片 serves 6

1 c. sliced cucumber

① {
1 c. water
1 t. salt
}

● Slice the cucumber and soak it in ① for 10 minutes; drain and serve.
■ The cucumbers may be rinsed if they are too salty. Season with other spices.

炒 菠 菜
Stir-fried spinach
Epinards sautés

炒 高 麗 菜
Stir-fried cabbage
Chou sauté

炒 豆 芽 菜
Stir-fried bean sprouts
Pousses de soja sautées

68

焗 三 蔬
Vegetable casserole
Chou au gratin

炸 茄 餅
Fried eggplant
Beignets d'aubergine

69

Stir-fried spinach 炒菠菜

1⅓ lb. spinach

① { 1   T. chopped garlic
2   T. water
1   t. salt
2   T. oil

❶ Wash the spinach and tear it into pieces 2 inches long.
❷ Heat the wok then add 2 T. oil. Stir-fry the spinach over high heat and add ① . Quickly stir-fry until thoroughly mixed. Serve.

Stir-fried cabbage 炒高麗菜

⅔   lb. cabbage
1   medium-size tomato
2   T. oil

① { 3   T. water
2   t. sugar
⅔   t. salt

❶ Cut the cabbage and tomato into bite-size pieces.
❷ Heat the wok then add 2 T. oil. Stir-fry the tomato lightly then add the cabbage; add ① Quickly stir-fry until thoroughly mixed. Serve.

Stir-fried bean sprouts 炒豆芽菜

⅔   lb. bean sprouts
2   T. oil
⅔   t. salt

● Wash the bean sprouts. Heat the wok then add 2 T. oil. Stir-fry the bean sprouts over high heat then add the salt. Quickly stir-fry the bean sprouts until thoroughly mixed. Serve.
■ If preparing this dish for guests, both ends of the bean sprouts may be removed. Use stems only.

Vegetable casserole   焗三蔬   serves 6

⅔ lb. nappa cabbage
½ lb. cauliflower
½ 1 lb. can asparagus or ½ lb. spinach
4 T. oil, butter or lard
6 T. flour

① { 1½ c. stock
1¼ t. salt
1 t. sugar }

1 T. butter or parmesan cheese (cut butter into small cubes)
6 T. oil

❶ Preheat the oven to 450°. Cut the cabbage into bite-size pieces and parboil it for 1 minute; remove and put in cold water. Cut the cauliflower into bite-size pieces and put them into boiling water; parboil for 2 minutes. Remove and drain.

❷ Heat the wok then add 6 T. oil. Brown the flour over low heat for 2 minutes; remove.

❸ Boil ① ; add the drained cabbage and cauliflower; cook for 4 minutes. Add the asparagus and cook for 1 minute. Drain (retain stock) and remove vegetables to casserole dish. Gradually add the stock to the flour and butter mixture (thickening). Pour the thickening over the vegetables. Sprinkle with butter, parmesan cheese, or finely chopped ham. Bake in 450° oven for 10 minutes; serve.

Fried eggplant   炸茄餅   serves 6

⅔ lb. Chinese eggplant
⅓ lb. ground meat, pork or beef
① { pinch of salt
½ T. cornstarch
1½ T. water }

② { 1 c. flour
1 c. water
½ t. baking powder }
oil for frying

❶ Cut off the ends of the eggplant then carefully cut it into diagonal, ¼-inch slices-cutting through every other slice to form a pocket (Fig. 1). Add ① to the meat; mix thoroughly until the ground meat is completely blended and smooth (filling). Mix ② to make a batter.

❷ Put some filling in each pocket (Fig. 2).

❸ Heat the wok over medium heat then add the oil for frying. Individually dip each sliced segment of eggplant in the batter then put them in the wok (Fig. 3). Depp-fry the eggplant segments for 2-3 minutes over high heat. Remove and drain. Serve with ketchup or Szechuan peppercorn salt.

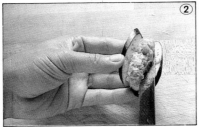

箱子豆腐
Stuffed bean curd
Carrés de fromage de soja farcis

芙蓉炒蛋
Egg foo yung
Œufs Foo-yung

72

豉汁豆腐
Spicy bean curd
Fromage de soja aux haricots noirs fermentés

家常豆腐
Family-style bean curd
Fromage de soja mode familiale

Stuffed bean curd　箱子豆腐　serves 6

8　pieces of bean curd (2 boxes)	6　½-inch pieces of green onion
oil for frying	② { 1½　c. stock
½　lb. ground meat, pork or beef	3　T. soy sauce
½　T. cooking wine or sherry	1　t. sugar }
① { 1½　T. water	③ { ½　T. cornstarch } mix
¼　t. salt	1½　T. water }
dash of pepper	1　T. chopped green onions
1　T. chopped green onion	1　T. oil
1　T. cornstarch	

❶ Add ① to the ground meat and mix thoroughly until it is completely blended and smooth. Add 1 T. onions and 1 T. cornstarch; mix (filling). Pat the bean curd to dry.

❷ Heat the wok then add the oil for frying. Deep-fry the bean curd until it is golden; remove. Allow the bean curd to cool slightly. Laterally, cut the bean curd to make a ¼-inch slice to about ¼-inch from the opposite edge (Fig. 1). (Do not slice through.) Scoop out the bean curd to form a pocket (Fig. 2) and fill it with meat filling (Fig. 3).

❸ Heat the wok then add 1 T. oil. Stir-fry the pieces of onion until fragrant. Add ② and the bean curd; cover. Cook over low heat for 8 minutes or until the liquid is reduced to ¾ cup. Add mixture ③ to thicken; stir. Sprinkle with chopped onion; serve.

①

②

③

Egg foo yung　芙蓉炒蛋　serves 6

5　eggs	② { ⅔　c. water
① { ¾　t. salt	¼　t. salt
½　t. sugar	1　t. cornstarch } mix
½　c. shelled shrimp	8　T. oil
1　slice of ham	
1　c. shredded brown onion	

❶ Lightly beat the eggs with ① . Devein and wash the shrimp; drain. Shred the ham.

❷ Heat the wok then add 3 T. oil. Stir-fry the shrimp until it changes color; remove. If necessary, add oil. Stir-fry the onions until tender; remove. Combine eggs, shrimp, onions, and shredded ham.

❸ Heat the wok over high heat then add 5 T. oil. Swirl the oil in the wok to cover the lower two-thirds of the wok. Pour the egg combination into the wok and quickly stir until the mixture solidifies (do not overcook). Lightly flatten to form a big pancake. If necessary, add a little more oil to prevent burning.Hold the wok and move it in a circular motion. Continue to cook the egg too yung until it is golden brown; flip it over to the uncooked side and cook to golden. Remove.

❹ Bring ② to a boil in a wok or saucepan; pour over the egg foo yung. Serve.

■ Sandwich ham may be used.

■ Shredded bamboo shoot or shredded black mushrooms may be added to the egg mixture.

Spicy bean curd 豉汁豆腐

1 box bean curd (4 pieces in a box)
① 1 T. green onion
½ T. ginger root } chopped
1 garlic clove
¼ c. shredded lean meat, pork, beef, or chicken
1½ T. fermented black beans

② 1 c. water
3 T. soy sauce
1 T. cooking wine or sherry

③ 1 T. cornstarch
1 T. water } mix
3 T. oil

❶ Cut the bean curd into bite-size pieces.
❷ Heat the wok then add 3 T. oil. Stir-fry ① until fragrant. Add the shredded meat and fermented black beans. Stir-fry lightly; add ② and the bean curd. Bring to a boil then lower the heat. Cook for 3 minutes. Add mixture ③ to thicken; stir. Serve.

Family-style bean curd 家常豆腐

2 pieces of bean curd (4 pieces in a box)
oil for frying
⅓ c. sliced meat: pork, beef, or chicken
① ½ T. soy sauce
1 t. cornstarch
2 presoftened mushrooms
½ c. sliced bamboo shoot
6 ½-inch pieces of green onion

6 slices of ginger root
1 t. hot chili paste
② 1⅓ c. stock
2 T. soy sauce
1 T. oyster sauce
1 t. sugar
③ ½ T. cornstarch
1½ T. water } mix

❶ Hold the cleaver so that the blade is parallel to the cutting surface. Cut each piece of bean curd into three slices. Diagonally cut the slices from corner to corner (to total 12 pieces) (Fig. 1); pat the slices dry (Fig. 2). Mix ① with the meat and marinate for 20 minutes. Slice the mushrooms.
❷ Heat the wok then add the oil. Dip the strainer in the oil to coat it lightly with oil; remove the strainer. Arrange the pieces of bean curd in the strainer. Place the strainer in the wok (Fig. 3); when the bean curd surfaces, after 2 to 3 minutes, remove and drain them. Remove the oil from the wok. Reheat the wok.
❸ Heat 2 T. oil and stir-fry the onions and ginger root until they are fragrant. Alternately add then stir the hot chili paste, mushrooms, and bamboo shoot. Add ② then add the bean curd; cook for 3 minutes. Add the pork and mixture ③ to thicken; stir. Remove and serve.
■ Hot chili paste may be substituted with hot red peppers or may be omitted.

蒸　　　蛋
Steamed egg pudding
Pudding salé aux œufs

白 菜 豆 腐
Chinese cabbage with bean curd
Chou au fromage de soja

八　寶　菜
Shrimp, meat, and vegetable dish
Légumes sautés huit trésors

佛手白菜
Cabbage rolls
Rouleaux de chou

Steamed egg pudding 蒸蛋 serves 6

① {
3 eggs
1 T. soy sauce
¾ t. salt
1 t. cooking wine or sherry
½ t. oil, sesame oil, or shortening
}
2 c. water

❶ Beat the eggs and mix with ① and water. Put them in a heatproof bowl or small casserole.

❷ Boil the water in a pan and steam the casserole for 2 minutes over high heat. Lower the heat and steam for another 15 minutes.

■ Test for doneness by inserting a toothpick or a chopstick in the center of the pudding. If the chopstick is clean when removed, the pudding is cooked. Maintain the low heat or the pudding will become hard if the heat is too high.

■ If the pudding is being baked, preheat the oven to 300°. Put one-half inch cold water in a shallow baking pan. Place the casserole dish in the pan of water and bake for 40 minutes. The steaming and baking time may vary due to the size of the casserole dish. Check for doneness regularly.

Nappa cabbage with bean curd 白菜豆腐 serves 6

1⅓ lbs. nappa cabbage
1 piece bean curd (4 pieces in a box)
2 scallops
1 slice of ham
3 T. oil

① {
soaking water or steaming broth retained from scallops, add stock
} to equal ¾ cup
¾ t. salt
dash of pepper

② { 1½ T. cornstarch
1½ T. water } mix

❶ Cut off the bottom of the cabbage; wash it and cut the leaves into bite-size pieces. Cut the bean curd into 1-inch cubes. Soak the scallops in hot water for 1 hour or steam them for 30 minutes, or until soft. Retain the liquid. Shred the scallops by hand. Cut the ham into bite-size pieces.

❷ Heat the wok then add 3 T. oil. Add the stem pieces of cabbage; stir briefly and add the leaves (Fig. 1). Add the bean curd, scallops, ham, and ① (Fig. 2); bring to a boil. Cover and cook over low heat for 4 minutes. Add mixture ② to thicken; stir (Fig. 3). Remove and serve.

■ Sandwich ham may be used.

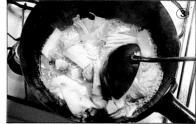

Shrimp, meat, and vegetable dish 八寶菜 serves 6

① {
⅓ c. shelled shrimp
dash of salt
½ t. cornstarch
}

② {
⅓ c. sliced lean meat, pork, beef, or chicken
dash of salt
½ t. cornstarch
}

2 presoftened Chinese black mushrooms
1 slice of ham
1 c. nappa cabbage
3 T. oil

¾ c. flowerets of broccoli, cauliflower, cut into bite-size pieces
⅓ c. sliced bamboo shoot

③ {
1 c. stock or water
1 T. cooking wine or sherry
1 t. sugar
¾ t. salt
dash of pepper
}

④ {
1 T. cornstarch
2 T. water
} mix

❶ Use a cleaver to cut the back of the shrimp lengthwise. Remove the dark vein. Place 1 t. salt and 1 T. water on the shrimp. Gently work the salt solution into the shrimp. Rinse with clear water. Rinse and drain the shrimp several times. And ① ; and ② to the sliced meat. Cut the ham into bite-size pieces.

❷ Separately parboil the cabbage (1 min.), broccoli (2 min.), and cauliflower (2 min.).

❸ Heat the wok then add 3 T. oil Separately stir-fry the shrimp and meat; remove. Bring ③ to a boil; add mushrooms, ham, cabbage, broccoli, cauliflower, and bamboo shoot and cook for 2 minutes. Return the shrimp and meet to the wok. Add mixture ④ to thicken; stir. Remove and serve.

Cabbage rolls 佛手白菜 serves 6

12 leaves of nappa cabbage
⅔ lb. ground meat: pork or beef

① {
1 T. cornstarch
3 T. water
½ t. salt
1 t. cooking wine or sherry
}

② {
steaming broth of the cabbage and stock } to equal 1 cup
1½ T. softened dry shrimps
½ T. soy sauce
½ t. salt
dash of pepper
}

③ {
½ T. cornstarch
1 T. water
} mix

❶ Parboil the cabbage leaves in boiling water for 1½ minutes, or until soft; remove and drain. Cut the stem of each leaf to 4 inches long. If the stem is thick, cut it lengthwise to make it pliable to roll (Fig. 1). Starting about 1/3-inch from the edge of the stem, make several cuts 2 inches long to 1/3-inch from the other edge (Figs. 2-3).

❷ Add ① to the meat and mix thoroughly until it is completely blended and smooth (filling). Divide into 12 portions.

❸ Sprinkle cornstarch on the stem of the cabbage leaf; crosswise place 1 portion of filling at one end of the stem. Roll up the leaf to enclose the filling. Follow same procedure for all cabbage stems. Place the cabbage rolls and pieces of cabbage retained in step 1 next to each other on a heatproof dish and steam over medium heat for 12 minutes. Remove steaming dish, retain liquid (to be used in ②). Line a serving dish with cabbage; place the cabbage rolls on top of the cabbage. Boil ② ; add mixture ③ to thicken; stir then pour over the cabbage rolls. Serve.

番茄炒飯
Fried rice with ground beef
Riz sauté sauce tomate

咖哩炒飯
Curried fried rice
Riz sauté au curry

蛋炒飯
Fried rice with egg
Riz sauté aux œufs

80

燴　　麺
Meat, shrimp, and noodle platter
Nouilles aux crevettes et à la viande

炒　　麺
Stir-fried noodles
Nouilles sautées

81

Fried rice with ground beef 番茄炒飯 serves 2

⅓ lb. ground beef
1   c. chopped brown onion
2½ c. steamed rice

① ⎰ 3 T. ketchup
   ⎱ 1 t. sugar
     ½ t. salt
     3 T. oil

- Heat the wok then add 3 T. oil. Saute the onions until fragrant. Add the ground beef and stir until it is cooked. Add the rice and ① ; stir-fry until the rice is fried. Serve.
- See below for directions to make steamed rice.

Curried fried rice 咖哩炒飯 serves 2

½   T. curry powder
½   c. shredded brown onion
½   t. salt
2½ c. steamed rice
3   T. oil

① ⎰ 2   slices ham or
   ⎰ ½   c. ham
   ⎱ ½   c. bell pepper   } shredded
     ¼   c. carrot

- Heat the wok then add 3 T. oil. Brown the curry powder; saute the onions. Add ① and lightly stir-fry. Add the rice and salt. Stir-fry until the rice is fried. Serve.
- See below for directions to steam the rice.

Fried rice with egg 蛋炒飯 serves 2

1   egg, beaten
6   shelled shrimp, leave tail intact
① ⎰ ⅓ c. diced botton mushrooms
   ⎰ 2 T. chopped green onions
   ⎱ 3 T. peas, fresh or frozen (thawed)

② ⎰ ½   t. salt
   ⎱ dash of pepper
     1¼ c. rice (equals 2½ c. steamed rice)
     3   T. oil

- Heat the wok then add 3 T. oil. Stir-fry the egg until it solidifies. Add ① and shrimp; lightly stir-fry. Add the steamed rice and ② . Stir-fry until the rice is fried. Serve.
- Method for preparing steamed rice. If a rice cooker is unavailable, rinse the rice (1¼ cups) until the water runs clear; drain. Put the rice and 1¼ cups water in a saucepan and let stand for about 30 minutes. Bring to a boil over high heat. Allow to boil for 1 minute. Cover with a tight-fitting lid; lower the heat and cook for 20 minutes. Turn off heat; let stand for 10 minutes.

Filling:
1⅓ lbs. ground meat (pork or beef)

① {
2 T. soy sauce
1 T. cooking wine or sherry
6 T. water
½ T. sesame oil
1 t. sugar
dash of pepper
}
1½ T. cornstarch

② {
3 T. chopped green onions
1½ T. chopped ginger root
}

Dough:
5 c. flour
¼ c. sugar

③ {
1¾ c. warm water
½ T. powdered yeast
}
2 T. oil or shortening

❶ Filling: Mix the meat with ① until it is completely blended and smooth, for about 5 minutes. Add the cornstarch and ② ; mix (filling).

❷ Dough: Put the warm water from ③ in a bowl; add the sugar and stir to dissolve it. Sprinkle the yeast into the bowl. Let it stand for 10 minutes. The yeast will form into a head and rise to the top. Sift the flour. Add the oil and mix them together with the water, sugar, and yeast mixture. Knead the dough into a ball. Remove the dough until it smooth and elastic then place it in a clean bowl and cover it with a damp cloth. Let it rise in a warm place for 1-4 hours or until it has doubled in bulk. The bowl may also be placed in a warm oven to stand for 1 hour.

❸ Procedure: Remove the dough from the bowl and knead it on a lightly floured surface until it is smooth and elastic. If the dough is too dry, add water; if it is too sticky, add flour. Roll the dough into a long, baton-like shape then divide it into 24 pieces. Flatten each piece with the palm of the hand. Place one portion of filling in the middle of the flattened dough. Wrap the dough to enclose the filling (Fig. 1). Shape the dough circle by pleating and pinching the edges (Fig. 2) to form the bun (Figs. 3, 4). Line the steamer with a damp cloth or small pieces of paper on which to set each bun. Let the buns stand for 10 minutes then steam them over high heat for 10 minutes. Steam heat the buns for later servings.

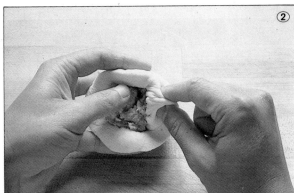

①

②

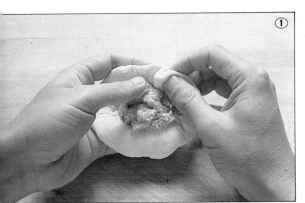

③

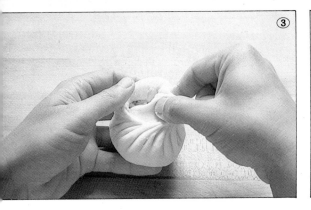

④

炸　餛　飩
Fried won ton
Raviolis Won ton frits

炸　春　捲
Fried egg rolls
Rouleaux de printemps

89

Filling:
⅓ lb. ground meat: pork, beef, or chicken

① {
1 T. water
1 t. cornstarch
½ t. salt
¼ t. cooking wine or sherry
2 drops of sesame oil
dash of pepper
}

30 won ton skins
oil for frying

❶ Filling: Add ① to the meat. Mix thoroughly until the meat is completely blended and smooth.

❷ Methods of wrapping the won ton:
Put 1 t. filling in the center of a won ton skin (Fig. 1). Diagonally fold the skin in half to form a triangle (Fig. 2); fold the edge containing the filling over about ½ inch (Fig. 3). Bring the two points together; moisten one inner edge and pinch the ends together to hold (Fig. 4).
OR
Place 1 T. filling across one end of the won ton skin. Make a flour and water paste. Roll the won ton over the filling; use some flour paste to moisten opposite edge to seal. A small sheet of dried sea weed may be placed on the won ton skin after adding the filling.

❸ Heat the wok then add the oil for frying. Deep-fry the won tons over medium heat until golden. Maintain medium heat. If the oil is too hot, the meat will be raw and the won ton skins may burn.

Won ton soup　餛飩湯　serves 6

● Boil 1½ cups stock. Pour the stock in a serving bowl and add: a dash of salt, pepper, 2 drops sesame oil, ½ T. soy sauce, and 1 T. chopped green onions. Boil water in a pan, gently drop some won tons and spinach into the water. Cook for 1 minute; remove and drain. Put won tons and spinach into the serving bowl; serve.

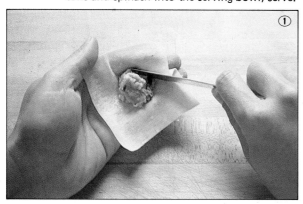
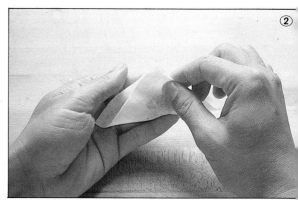
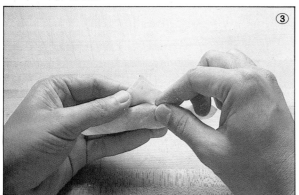
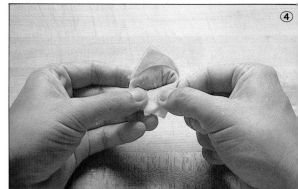

Filling:
½   c. shredded meat: pork loin, beef, or chicken (about ¼ lb.)

① { 1   t. cooking wine or sherry
    1   t. cornstarch
    ¼   t. salt

② { 4   c. shredded cabbage
    1   c. shredded celery
    ½   c. shredded carrot

③ { 1   T. sugar
    1   t. salt
    ¼   t. pepper
    1   t. sesame oil

16   egg roll skins

④ { 2   T. flour } flour paste
    2   T. water

oil for frying

⑤ { 2   T. soy sauce
    2   T. white vinegar
    1   T. shredded ginger root

❶ Add ① to the shredded pork and mix thoroughly. Heat the wok then 4 T. oil; stir-fry the pork until the color changes. Remove and drain (see p. 9 for precooking).

❷ Put the ingredients in ② in boiling water and cook for 10 seconds; remove and drain the vegetables. Add the pork and ③; toss lightly. Divide the mixture into 16 portions (filling).

❸ To wrap the egg rolls: Place the egg roll skin on working surface with one of the points on the top. Place a portion of filling in the middle of the egg roll skin (Fig. 1). Fold lower third of the egg roll skin over the filling to one-third from the top point (Fig. 2). Fold in the two ends and wrap the filling (Fig. 3). Moisten the top edge of the egg roll skin with mixture ④. Continue to wrap the egg roll skin to form a baton. Rolls should be about 4 inches long.

❹ Heat the wok then add the oil. Heat the oil for deep-frying. Deepfry the egg rolls over medium heat for 4 minutes, or until they are golden brown; remove and drain. Combine ingredients of ⑤ and use as a dipping sauce.

■ The vegetables in the filling may be varied according to individual taste.

■ The egg rolls skins may be purchased at most Chinese markets. If the egg roll skins are frozen, allow them to thaw out to room temperature. Separate each sheet and use.

八　寶　飯
Rice pudding
Gâteau de riz glutineux

杏仁豆腐
Chinese almond jello
Gelée aux amandes

Rice pudding 八寶飯

1 c. candied fruit of individual preference	½ c. red bean paste
2 c. glutinous rice	② { 1 c. water
1 T. lard, shortening, or butter	3 T. sugar
① { 3 T. sugar	③ { 1½ T. water } mix
2 T. lard, shortening, or butter	2 t. cornstarch

❶ Grease a heatproof bowl, 7″ x 3″, with 1 T. lard or shortening. Arrange the candied fruit in a circular fashion as shown (Fig. 1).

❷ Cook the rice as directed below. While rice is hot, mix with ① ; place one half of the rice into the prepared bowl (Fig. 2). Pack the rice firmly so that it lines the sides of the bowl. Leave an indentation in the middle; fill the indentation with red bean paste (Fig. 3). Add the rest of the rice (Fig. 4). Pack down rice again. Use a spoon, dipped in water, to make the surface smooth. (The water will prevent the rice from sticking to the spoon.) Steam over medium heat for 1 hour; remove. Place a serving dish on the bowl and invert them to remove the rice from the bowl.

❸ Bring ② to a boil. After the sugar dissolves, add mixture ③ to thicken; stir. Pour mixture over the rice pudding and serve.

■ To prepare red bean paste, see p. 102. Red bean paste may be purchased at most Chinese markets. If bean paste is not sweetened, add sugar to taste and mix.

■ If a rice cooker is not available: rinse 2 cups glutinous rice with water until the water runs clear. Put 1½ cups water in a pan; add the rice and let stand for about 30 minutes. Bring to a boil over high heat. Allow to boil for 1 minute. Cover with a tight-fitting lid. Hereafter, do not uncover rice until cooking time has elapsed. Cook for 20 minutes over low heat; turn off the heat and let stand for 10 minutes.

¼ oz. agar-agar (Fig. 1)
6 c. water
1 c. sugar

¾ c. evaporated milk
1 T. almond extract
1 1 lb. can fruit (individual preference)

- Lightly rinse the agar-agar (Fig. 2) then place it in a saucepan. Add 6 cups water and soak for 30 minutes. Heat until the agar-agar dissolves. Add the sugar and bring to a boil. Add the milk and almond extract (Fig. 3). Turn off the heat. Pour into a serving bowl or individual serving bowls (Fig. 4). Refrigerate until the mixture sets. Add fruit before serving.
- Agar-agar may be purchased at most Chinese markets. If unavailable, use gelatin and follow directions on package.

燒　賣 (一)
Shau mai
Shau mai I

96

燒賣 (二)
Shau mai II
Shau mai

97

Filling:
1   lb. ground meat, pork or beef
① ⎧ 4   T. water
   | 1½ T. soy sauce
   | ¾   T. cooking wine or sherry
   | ½   t. sugar
   | ¾   t. sesame oil
   ⎩ dash of pepper
   1½ T. cornstarch

Dough:
2½ c. flour
② ⎧ ½   c. boiling water
   | ¼   c. water
   ⎩ 1   T. oil or shortening

❶ Filling: Add ① to the meat; mix thoroughly until the meat is well blended and smooth. Add the cornstarch; mix. Divide into 30 portions.

❷ Dough: Put 2 c. flour in a mixing bowl. Remaining flour is used for hands if they become sticky. Add the boiling water from ② ; mix. Add the water and oil. Mix to form dough; knead into a smooth dough. Roll the dough into a long, baton-like shape and cut it into 30 pieces. Use a rolling pin to roll each portion into a thin 2-inch circle.

❸ Procedure: Place 1 portion of filling in the middle of the dough circle. Bring the opposite edges together and pinch them together to hold (Figs.1, 2). Shape loops, similar to a four-leaf clover (Fig. 3). Loops may be filled with grated carrots, a small leaf of parsley, chopped black mushroom, chopped hard boiled egg yolk (Fig. 4), or finely chopped green onion. Line the steamer with a damp cloth. Set the shau mai about 1 inch apart. Steam over high heat for 5 minutes; remove and serve.

■ The skin may be folded in various ways (see picture on p. 96).

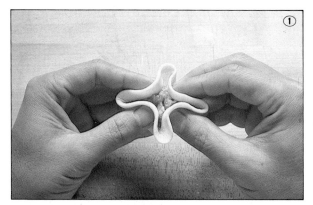
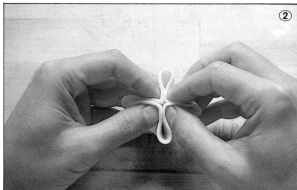
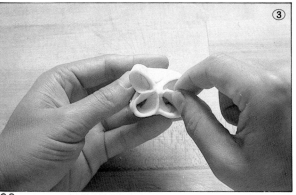
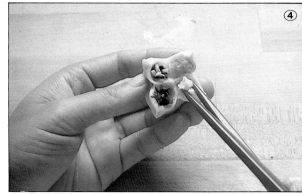

①
- 1 lb. ground meat: pork or beef
- 1½ T. soy suace
- ¾ T. cooking wine or sherry
- ¾ T. sesame oil
- ½ t. sugar
- dash of pepper
- 1 egg white

- 1½ T. cornstarch
- 30 won ton skins

❶ Filling: Add ① to meat and mix thoroughly until meat is well blended and smooth. Add cornstarch; mix. Divide into 30 portions.

❷ Skins: Cut off the edges of the won ton skins to form circles.

❸ Procedures: Place 1 portion of filling in the center of the won ton skin (Fig 1). Gather the edges of the won ton skin around the meat filling. Dip a teaspoon in water and use to smooth the surface of the meat (the water will prevent the meat from sticking to the spoon). Shau Mai may be garnished by placing a green pea on top (Fig. 2). A shrimp may be placed on top of the meat filling (Fig. 3). Gather the edges to form a waist. The tail of the shrimp should extend out of the filling (Fig. 4). Line the steamer with a damp cloth or oil it lightly. Steam over high heat for 5 minutes; remove and serve.

■ Won ton skins may be folded in various ways (see picture on p. 97).

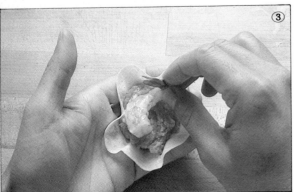

廣 式 月 餅
Cantonese-style moon cakes
Galettes de la lune (mode cantonnaise)

100

蘇 式 月 餅
Short moon cakes
Galettes de la lune (mode de Jiangsu)^I

杏 仁 酥
Chinese aimond cookies
Palets aux amandes

酥 餅
Short moon cakes
Galettes de la lune II

101

Filling:
20 salty egg yolks
2 ⅔ lb. red bean paste
Dough:
① { 4 C. flour
½ c. powdered milk
1 T. baking powder }

② { 3 eggs
1¼ c. sugar }
③ { ¾ c. butter
½ t. salt }
1 egg yolk
1 press or mold

Preheat oven to 350°.

❶ Filling: Place the egg yolks on a cookie sheet and bake for 15 minutes; remove. Divide the red bean paste into 20 portions. Put 1 egg yolk into 1 portion of the bean paste; use hands to roll it so that the bean paste covers the egg yolk.

❷ Dough: Beat ② for 10 minutes. Add ③ then add ① ; lightly mix well. Divide the mixture into 20 portions.

❸ Procedure: Preheat the oven to 400°. Take 1 portion of dough and flatten it, with the palms of hands, to a 4-inch circle. Place 1 portion of filling in the center of the dough circle and wrap it to enclose the filling. Pinch the edges to seal them. Roll the dough to a smooth surface. Lightly flour the mold and place the filled dough into the mold (Fig. 1); press the dough to fill the mold. If using a cookie press, gently tap it to loosen the dough (Fig. 2). Place the dough on a cookie sheet and brush egg yolk on top of the dough. Bake for 30 minutes.

■ Salty egg yolks may be purchased at most Chinese markets. Salty egg yolks are prepared so that the yolk will harden but the egg white remains runny. Remove the egg white before using.

■ Prepare the red bean paste as directed below. The canned red bean paste may be purchased at most Chinese markets.

■ The Cantonese cookie press is a special press that makes designs (as shown). The cookie press may be purchased through Wei-Chuan's Cooking. If the press is unavailable, use a chopstick or knife to score a checkerboard design on the dough.

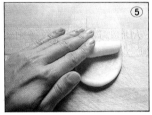

Method for making red bean paste 豆沙做法

Methods for making red bean paste:
Method A: Clean 1 1/3 lbs. red beans and place them in a deep pan. Add water to cover and cook for 2 minutes. Drain and discard the water. This preliminary cooking will eliminate the bitter taste. Put 10 cups of water in a pressure cooker and cook the beans for 25 minutes over medium heat. Strain the beans and discard the less (skins); retain the liquid. Pour the retained liquid and beans into a cloth pocket; squeeze out excess water. Put ½ cup lard, 2 cups sugar, and dried bean paste in a wok. Stir to mix thoroughly. Stir continuously to prevent the paste from sticking to the wok. Cook for about 10 minutes, or until the liquid has almost completely evaporated. Let cool. Red bean paste may be used to make various kinds of snacks (1 1/3 lbs. of red beans is about 2 1/6 lbs. of red bean paste.)
Method B: Similar process as in Method A except omit straining the beans.

■ If canned sweetened red bean paste is used, add 2 T. lard and cook for 10 minutes. Red bean paste is ready for use when cool.